SIMPLY
DELICIOUS

VEGETARIAN

SIMPLY
DELICIOUS

VEGETARIAN

Carla Bardi

Zak
BOOKS

Zak Books is an imprint of McRae Publishing, Ltd.

Simply Delicious Vegetarian
was created and produced by McRae Publishing Ltd, London
info@mcraebooks.com
Publishers: Anne McRae and Marco Nardi
Project Director: Anne McRae
Design: Sara Mathews
Text: Carla Bardi
Photography: Studio Marco Lanza
Home Economist: Benedetto Rillo
Artbuying: McRae Publishing Ltd
Layouts: Aurora Granata
Repro: Fotolito Raf, Florence
Pre-press: Filippo Delle Monache

ISBN: 978-1-4351-0200-2

Manufactured in China

6 8 10 9 7 5

Table of Contents

SALADS

Strawberry Salad
with cucumber and brown rice

Place the strawberries in a large bowl and drizzle with the balsamic vinegar.

Mix the yogurt and mint in a medium bowl. Stir in the oil and season with salt. Refrigerate until ready to use.

Wash the salad and dry well. Place in a large salad bowl. Arrange the rice on top of the salad, followed by the strawberries and cucumber.

Spoon the yogurt sauce over the top. Season with pepper and serve.

10 oz (300 g) strawberries, rinsed, hulled, and thinly sliced
1 tablespoon balsamic vinegar
1 cup (250 ml) low-fat yogurt
1 tablespoon finely chopped mint
3 tablespoons walnut oil
Salt and freshly ground pink (or black) pepper
8 oz (250 g) mixed salad greens
1 cup (200 g) cooked brown rice
1 cucumber, thinly sliced

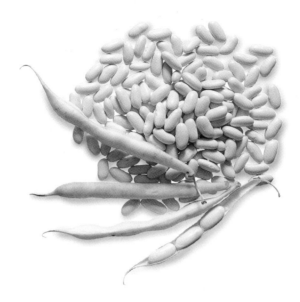

SERVES 4–6

PREPARATION 15 min + 30 min to rest

COOKING 30 min

DIFFICULTY level 1

Bean Salad
with onion and bell pepper

Place the beans in a large bowl. Add the bell pepper, onion, garlic, and parsley and toss well.

Beat the oil and lemon juice in a small bowl with a fork. Season with salt and pepper.

Drizzle the dressing over the salad. Toss well, cover, and let rest for 30 minutes.

Arrange the salad greens in a large salad bowl. Spoon the bean salad over the top. Garnish with the sprigs of parsley and serve.

1 (14-oz/400-g) can cranberry or borlotti beans, drained

1 (14-oz/400-g) can cannellini or white-kidney beans, drained

1 large red bell pepper (capsicum), seeded and finely sliced

1 sweet red onion, thinly sliced

1 clove garlic, finely chopped

4 tablespoons finely chopped parsley + extra sprigs, to garnish

1/4 cup (60 ml) extra-virgin olive oil

Freshly squeezed juice of 1 lemon

Salt and freshly ground black pepper

5 oz (150 g) lollo rosso (or other) salad greens

Arugula Salad
with pear, brie, and walnuts

Beat the oil, vinegar, and salt with a fork in a small bowl to make a smooth dressing.

Arrange the arugula in a large salad bowl. Arrange the brie on the arugula. Top with the slices of pear.

Drizzle with the dressing. Sprinkle with walnuts and serve at once.

1/4 cup (60 ml) extra-virgin olive oil
2 tablespoons balsamic vinegar
Salt
5 oz (150 g) arugula (rocket) leaves
8 oz (200 g) brie, sliced
3 large ripe pears, cored and sliced
16–20 walnuts, coarsely chopped

Spelt Salad
with mozzarella and corn

Cook the spelt in a large pot of salted boiling water until tender, 35–40 minutes. Drain well and cool under cold running water. Drain again and transfer to a clean kitchen cloth. Dry well and place in a large salad bowl.

While the spelt is cooking, preheat the broiler (grill) to high. Grill the bell pepper, turning often, until it is charred all over, 15–20 minutes. Wrap the blackened bell pepper in aluminum foil and let rest for 10 minutes. Unwrap and remove the skin and seeds. Rinse under cold water, dry well, and slice thinly.

Add the bell pepper, mozzarella, corn, parsley, basil, marjoram, and garlic to the salad bowl with the spelt. Toss well.

Beat the oil and lemon juice in a small bowl with a fork. Season with salt and pepper. Drizzle the dressing over the salad. Toss well before serving.

1 lb (500 g) spelt (or pearl barley)
1 large red bell pepper (capsicum)
8 oz (250 g) fresh mozzarella cheese, drained and cut into small cubes
4 oz (125 g) canned corn (sweetcorn)
1 tablespoon finely chopped parsley
1 tablespoon finely chopped basil
1/2 tablespoon finely chopped marjoram
1 clove garlic, finely chopped
1/3 cup (90 ml) extra-virgin olive oil
Freshly squeezed juice of 1 lemon
Salt and freshly ground black pepper

Pineapple Salad
with peanuts and bean sprouts

Place the pineapple, bean sprouts, peanuts, carrots, and spring onions in a large salad bowl. Toss gently.

Place the peanut butter, oil, soy sauce, vinegar, and chile in a small saucepan over low heat. Stir gently until well mixed, adding enough water to obtain a smooth, creamy dressing.

Spoon the dressing over the salad, or serve separately in a small bowl so that guests can help themselves.

8 oz (250 g) fresh or canned pineapple, cut in bite-size pieces
8 oz (250 g) bean sprouts
1 cup (100 g) toasted peanuts
2 large carrots, grated
1 small cucumber, peeled and diced
2 spring onions, finely sliced
6 tablespoons smooth peanut butter
2 tablespoons vegetable oil
2 teaspoons light soy sauce
1 teaspoon white vinegar
1 teaspoon ground chile (or 1 fresh red chile pepper, finely sliced)
About $1/2$ cup (125 ml) cold water

Orange Salad
with artichokes

Clean the artichokes by trimming the stalks and cutting off the top third of the leaves. Remove the tough outer leaves by pulling them down and snapping them off at the base. Cut the artichokes in half and use a sharp knife to remove any fuzzy core. Cut the artichokes into thin wedges.

Place the artichokes in a large salad bowl and drizzle with half the lemon juice. Add the oranges, pecorino, and parsley. Drizzle with the oil and remaining lemon juice and season with salt and pepper.

Toss well and serve.

6 artichokes
Freshly squeezed juice of I lemon
2 oranges, peeled and cut into segments
3 oz (90 g) aged pecorino cheese, flaked
I tablespoon finely chopped parsley
$1/3$ cup (90 ml) extra-virgin olive oil
Salt and freshly ground black pepper

Baked Rice Salad
with peas, green beans, and corn

Preheat the oven to 350°F (180°C/gas 4). Stud the onion with the cloves.

Heat 2 tablespoons of the oil in a large Dutch oven or casserole over medium heat. Add the onion and sauté until softened, 3–4 minutes.

Add the rice and mix well. Add the bay leaf and stock. Cover and bake in the oven until the rice has absorbed all the stock and is al dente, about 20 minutes. Remove from the oven and let cool.

Meanwhile, cook the green beans in a medium pot of salted boiling water until just tender, 5–7 minutes. Drain well and let cool.

Cook the peas in a small pot of salted boiling water until just tender, 3–5 minutes. Drain well and let cool.

Preheat the broiler (grill) to high. Grill the bell pepper, turning often, until charred all over, 15–20 minutes. Wrap the blackened bell pepper in aluminum foil and let rest for 10 minutes. Unwrap and remove the skin and seeds. Rinse under cold water, dry well, and slice thinly.

Place the gherkins, capers, remaining oil, and vinegar in a food processor. Blend until smooth.

Transfer the rice to a large salad bowl. Remove and discard the onion, cloves, and bay leaf. Add the green beans, peas, corn, pepper, and arugula.

Drizzle with the dressing and toss gently. Serve lukewarm.

1 small onion
3 cloves
1/3 cup (90 ml) extra-virgin olive oil
1 1/2 cups (300 g) short-grain rice
1 bay leaf
Generous 2 1/3 cups (600 ml) vegetable stock, boiling
5 oz (150 g) fresh or frozen green beans, chopped
5 oz (150 g) fresh or frozen peas
1 large red pepper (capsicum)
6 pickled gherkins, drained and chopped
1 tablespoon salt-cured capers, rinsed
3 tablespoons white wine vinegar
Salt
5 oz (150 g) canned corn (sweetcorn)
4 oz (125 g) arugula (rocket), chopped

Potato Salad
with cherry tomatoes and olives

Cook the potatoes in a large pot of salted boiling water until tender, about 20 minutes. Drain well and let cool slightly.

Place the olives in a large salad bowl. Add the basil, garlic, and vinegar, and mix well.

Cut the potatoes in half and and add to the salad bowl. Toss gently and let cool completely.

Add the celery and tomatoes. Drizzle with oil and season with salt. Toss again and serve.

2 lb (1 kg) new potatoes
1 cup (100 g) green olives, pitted
1 cup (100 g) black olives, pitted
2 tablespoons finely chopped basil
1 clove garlic, finely chopped
1 tablespoon white wine vinegar
1 heart celery, sliced
16 cherry tomatoes, halved
$1/4$ cup (60 ml) extra-virgin olive oil
Salt

SERVES 6

PREPARATION 20–25 min

COOKING 15 min

DIFFICULTY level 2

Grilled Salad

Grill the bell peppers, tomatoes, garlic, and chile pepper, if using, on the barbecue or in a grill pan until the skins of the bell peppers are blackened, about 15 minutes.

Seal the bell peppers in a paper bag for 10 minutes to make it easier to remove the skins. Peel the bell peppers and tomatoes while still warm. Cut away the tough parts and remove the seeds.

Coarsely mash the bell peppers, chile pepper, tomatoes, and garlic. Add the mashed hard-boiled eggs, celery, parsley, capers, and cilantro.

Mix the oil and lemon juice in a small bowl. Drizzle over the vegetables. Garnish with the remaining egg quarters and olives.

- 6 green bell peppers (capsicums)
- 4 large ripe tomatoes
- 4 cloves garlic, lightly crushed but whole
- 1 fresh red chile pepper, finely chopped (optional)
- 4 hard-boiled eggs, 3 mashed + 1 cut into quarters
- 2 stalks celery, finely chopped
- 1 sprig parsley, finely chopped
- 1 tablespoons salt-cured capers
- 1 tablespoon finely chopped cilantro (coriander)
- 3 tablespoons extra-virgin olive oil
- 1 tablespoon freshly squeezed lemon juice
- 1 cup (100 g) black olives, to garnish

Rice Salad
with garbanzo beans and tomatoes

Cook the rice in a large pot of salted, boiling water with 1 tablespoon of oil until tender, 12–15 minutes. Drain and let cool completely. Transfer the rice to a large bowl.

Mix the remaining oil, vinegar, and red pepper flakes in a small bowl. Pour the dressing over the rice and toss well.

Mix half the tomatoes and half the garbanzo beans into the rice. Add the mint and mix well. Season with salt. Top the rice salad with the remaining tomatoes and garbanzo beans. Garnish with a sprig of mint.

2½ cups (500 g) short-grain rice
¼ cup (60 ml) extra-virgin olive oil
2 tablespoons red wine vinegar
⅛ teaspoon red pepper flakes
1 lb (500 g) cherry tomatoes, thinly sliced
3 cups (300 g) canned garbanzo beans (chickpeas), drained
1 bunch mint, torn + extra, to garnish
Salt

Arugula Salad
with parmesan and red apple

Place the arugula in a large salad bowl. Top with the Parmesan.

Cut the apple in half, remove the core, and cut into small dice. Drizzle with the lemon juice and add to the salad. Sprinkle with the walnuts.

Place the oil, vinegar, and mustard in a small bowl. Season with salt and pepper and beat with a fork until well mixed.

Drizzle the dressing over the salad. Toss gently and serve at once.

6 oz (180 g) arugula (rocket)
4 oz (125 g) Parmesan, in flakes
1 large red Delicious apple
Freshly squeezed juice of $1/2$ lemon
16 walnuts, coarsely chopped
$1/4$ cup (60 ml) extra-virgin olive oil
2 tablespoons white wine vinegar
1 teaspoon French mustard
Salt and freshly ground black pepper

Pasta Salad

with feta, garlic, and black olives

Place the tomatoes, onion, garlic, feta, oil, basil, mint, and lemon zest in a large salad bowl. Toss well and season with salt and pepper. Let rest for 30 minutes.

Cook the pasta in a large pot of salted boiling water until al dente. Drain well and cool under cold running water. Drain again and dry on a clean kitchen cloth.

Add the pasta to the bowl with the tomato and cheese mixture. Add the olives and toss well. Garnish with basil and serve.

1½ lb (750 g) cherry tomatoes, quartered
1 small red onion, finely sliced
1 clove garlic, finely chopped
8 oz (250 g) feta cheese, cut into small cubes
⅓ cup (90 ml) extra-virgin olive oil
1 tablespoon finely chopped basil
    + extra sprigs, to garnish
1 tablespoon finely chopped mint
Grated zest of 1 lemon
Salt and freshly ground black pepper
1 lb (500 g) penne or other short pasta shape
1 cup (100 g) black olives, pitted

Moroccan Salad

Soak the spring onions in a bowl of iced water for 10 minutes to lose their pungent flavor. Drain and slice in thin rings.

Wash and chop the arugula and place in a large bowl. Add the radishes, oranges, olives, spring onions, and walnuts.

Dressing: Beat the orange juice and oil with a pinch of salt and pepper. Add the lemon juice, orange flower water, and cinnamon and mix until blended. Drizzle over the salad and serve.

3 spring onions, white parts only
1 bunch arugula (rocket)
1 bunch radishes, washed and thinly sliced
3 oranges, peeled and thinly sliced
2/3 cup (60 g) pitted black olives
15–20 shelled walnuts, coarsely chopped

Dressing
1/4 cup (60 ml) freshly squeezed orange juice
1/3 cup (90 ml) extra-virgin olive oil
Salt and freshly ground black pepper
Freshly squeezed juice of 1 lemon
1 tablespoon orange flower water
1/8 teaspoon ground cinnamon

Fusilli Salad

with peas and hazelnuts

Cook the pasta in a large pot of salted boiling water until al dente. Drain well and cool under cold running water. Drain again and dry on a clean kitchen towel. Transfer to a large salad bowl.

Cook the peas in a large pot of salted boiling until tender, about 5 minutes. Drain well and cool under cold running water. Drain well and add to the bowl with the pasta.

Beat the oil and mustard in a small bowl with a fork.

Drizzle over the salad and season with salt and pepper. Toss well. Add the hazelnuts and pecorino and toss again. Garnish with parsley and serve.

1 lb (500 g) fusilli
2 cups (300 g) fresh or frozen peas
1/4 cup (60 ml) extra-virgin olive oil
1 tablespoon French mustard
Salt and freshly ground black pepper
1/3 cup (50 g) chopped hazelnuts
5 oz (150 g) aged pecorino cheese, cut into flakes
1 tablespoon finely chopped parsley, to garnish

SERVES 4

PREPARATION 15 min

COOKING 15 min

DIFFICULTY level 1

Fusilli Salad

with cherry tomatoes and ricotta

Cook the pasta in a large pot of salted boiling water until al dente. Drain well and cool under cold running water. Drain again and dry on a clean kitchen towel. Transfer to a large salad bowl.

Beat the ricotta, oil, garlic, and basil in a large salad bowl to make a smooth dressing. Season with salt and pepper. Mix well.

Add the pasta and tomatoes to the bowl with the dressing. Toss well. Garnish with basil and serve.

1 lb (500 g) fusilli
12 oz (350 g) ricotta cheese, drained
1/3 cup (90 ml) extra-virgin olive oil
1 clove garlic, finely chopped
20 basil leaves, torn + extra, to garnish
Salt and freshly ground black pepper
20 cherry tomatoes, halved

Cheese Salad
with fresh fruit and herbs

Place both cheeses in a large salad bowl. Add the lettuce, radicchio, endive, apple, pear, grapes, sultanas, orange, and grapefruit. Toss well.

Beat the oil and vinegar in a small bowl with a fork. Add the mustard, dill, chives, parsley, and tarragon. Season with salt and pepper and beat again.

Drizzle the salad with the dressing and toss gently. Serve at once.

4 oz (125 g) emmental or other mild cheese, cut into small cubes

4 oz (125 g) aged pecorino or Parmesan cheese cut into flakes

4 oz (125 g) romaine lettuce, chopped

1 small radicchio, shredded

1 head curly endive, chopped

1 apple, peeled, cored, and cut into small cubes

1 pear, peeled, cored, and cut into small cubes

3 oz (90 g) green grapes, halved

2 tablespoons golden raisins (sultanas)

1 orange, peeled and cut in segments

1 pink grapefruit, peeled and cut in segments

1 shallot, finely chopped

1/4 cup (60 ml) extra-virgin olive oil

1 tablespoon balsamic vinegar

1 tablespoon wholegrain mustard

2 tablespoons finely chopped dill

2 tablespoons finely chopped chives

2 tablespoons finely chopped parsley

1 tablespoon finely chopped tarragon

Salt and freshly ground white pepper

Gado Gado

Wash and dry the lettuce and use it to line a salad bowl. Arrange the potato, beans, cabbage, and bean sprouts on top.

Cover with alternate slices of tomato and hard-boiled egg and arrange the onion rings, spring onions, and chile pepper on top. Sprinkle with the parsley.

Heat the oil in an omelet pan and pour in the beaten eggs, spreading thinly across the bottom. Cook until firm, then remove and set aside to cool. Cut into thin shreds and pile in the center of the salad.

Add the pineapple chunks and shrimp crisps, if liked, then toss all the ingredients gently (otherwise leave them separate).

Sauce: Place all the sauce ingredients in a small, heavy-bottomed saucepan over medium-low heat and bring to a boil, stirring constantly. Set aside to cool.

Pour over the salad or serve in a separate bowl.

1 crisp lettuce

2 large cooked potatoes, sliced

8 oz (250 g) lightly cooked green beans, sliced

8 oz (250 g) shredded cabbage, blanched

5 oz (150 g) fresh bean sprouts

15 cherry tomatoes, cut in half

3 hard-boiled eggs, shelled and sliced

1 onion, sliced

2 spring onions, chopped

1–2 fresh red chile peppers, seeded and shredded

2 tablespoons finely chopped parsley

1 tablespoon extra-virgin olive oil

2 eggs, beaten

$1/4$ teaspoon salt

$1/2$ cup fresh pineapple chunks

1 cup shrimp crisps (optional)

Sauce

1 tablespoon soy sauce

1 tablespoon lemon juice

6 tablespoons crunchy peanut butter

1 teaspoon red pepper flakes

$1/2$ teaspoon salt

2 teaspoons sugar

$3/4$ cup (180 ml) thick coconut milk

2 tablespoons extra-virgin olive oil

Spinach Salad
with parmesan and grapefruit

Rinse the spinach leaves thoroughly under cold running water and dry well. Remove any roots or tough stems.

Arrange the spinach on four individual serving plates. Top with the Parmesan and grapefruit.

Mix the lemon juice, oil, and chives in a small bowl. Season with salt and pepper. Pour the dressing over the salads and serve.

8 oz (250 g) fresh baby spinach leaves
4 oz (125 g) Parmesan cheese, in flakes
1 grapefruit, cut into segments
Freshly squeezed juice of $\frac{1}{2}$ lemon
3 tablespoons extra-virgin olive oil
1 tablespoon finely chopped chives
Salt and freshly ground black pepper

Rice Salad

with olives and raisins

Cook the rice in a large pot of salted, boiling water until tender but still firm, about 15 minutes.

Drain and pass under cold running water for 30 seconds to stop the cooking process. Drain again and dry well on a clean cloth. Transfer to a large salad bowl.

Drizzle with the oil and lemon juice. Season with pepper. Add the remaining ingredients and toss well.

1½ cups (300 g) short-grain rice

⅓ cup (90 ml) extra-virgin olive oil

1½ tablespoons freshly squeezed lemon juice

Salt and freshly ground white pepper

4 medium tomatoes, diced

2 stalks celery, sliced

6 pickled gherkins, sliced

8 small white pickled onions, quartered

1 tablespoon salt-cured capers, drained

10 green olives in brine, pitted and quartered

2 tablespoons golden raisins (sultanas), rinsed and drained

4 oz (125 g) Parmesan cheese, flaked

SOUPS

Cool Melon Soup

Cut the melons in half horizontally. Scoop out the flesh with a spoon, leaving a ½-inch (1-cm) border. Place the flesh in a bowl. Reserve the melon shells.

Chop the cardamom, basil, chile, garlic, and dill in a food processor until they form a smooth pesto (sauce).

Add the melon flesh, oil, and salt to the food processor with the pesto and process until smooth.

Add the lemon juice and Worcestershire sauce and stir until well blended.

Spoon the soup into the reserved melon shells and chill in the refrigerator for I hour before serving.

2 small cantaloupe (rock melons), weighing about 2 lb (I kg) each
Seeds of 6 cardamom pods
2 leaves fresh basil, torn
I small chile pepper, seeded and finely chopped
½ clove garlic
I bunch fresh dill or chervil, finely chopped
I tablespoon extra-virgin olive oil
½ teaspoon salt
I tablespoon fresh lemon juice
I teaspoon Worcestershire sauce

SERVES 4–6

PREPARATION 15 min

DIFFICULTY level 1

Tomato Soup

with yogurt

Blanch the tomatoes in a large pot of salted boiling water for 1 minute. Drain, run under cold water, and peel. Run through a vegetable mill or chop with a knife until smooth and then strain to remove the seeds.

Place the tomato purée in a medium saucepan over medium heat. Bring to a boil and season with the salt and pepper. Add the oregano.

Stir in the yogurt until well blended, reserving 1 tablespoon to garnish. Bring to a boil and simmer over low heat for 2–3 minutes. Sprinkle with half the basil and simmer for 2 minutes more.

Serve in individual soup bowls, garnished with the remaining basil and dotted with the yogurt. Serve with freshly baked bread or warm toast.

3 lb (1.5 kg) firm-ripe tomatoes
Salt and freshly ground black pepper
$\frac{1}{2}$ teaspoon dried oregano
2 cups (500 ml) plain yogurt
Fresh marjoram or oregano, to garnish
Fresh bread or toast, to serve

Butternut Soup

Melt the butter in a large saucepan over medium heat. Add the onions, garlic, salt, cumin, coriander, and mustard and sauté until the onions are tender, about 5 minutes.

Add the squash, potato, honey, chile, and ginger. Pour in 4 cups (1 liter) of the stock and bring to a boil over low heat. Cover and simmer until the vegetables have softened, about 15 minutes.

Add the beans, remaining 2 cups (500 ml) of stock, and half the lemon juice. Simmer for 5 minutes. Remove from the heat and let cool slightly.

Blend with a handheld blender until smooth. Return the pan to the heat and reheat gently, adding the remaining lemon juice and more stock if needed. Season with salt, pepper, and cayenne.

Swirl in the yogurt and garnish with the red bell pepper. Serve hot.

2 tablespoons butter – unsalted
2 small onions, finely chopped
1 clove garlic, finely chopped
1 teaspoon salt – Sea
½ teaspoon ground cumin
½ teaspoon ground coriander seeds
½ teaspoon dry mustard powder
2 medium butternut squash, peeled, seeded, and cut into small cubes
1 sweet potato or white potato, cubed
1 teaspoon honey
1 green chile pepper, finely chopped
1-inch (2.5-cm) piece fresh ginger, peeled and finely chopped
6 cups (1.5 liters) chicken stock   4 cups Veg St
2 cups (400 g) canned garbanzo beans (chickpeas)
Freshly squeezed juice of 2 lemons
Salt and freshly ground black pepper
½ teaspoon cayenne pepper – No
½ cup (125 ml) plain yogurt – NO
2 tablespoons diced red bell pepper (capsicum)

SERVES 4
PREPARATION 35 min
COOKING 30 min
DIFFICULTY level 2

Mushroom Soup
with sherry

Béchamel Sauce: Melt the butter in a medium heavy-bottomed saucepan over low heat. Add the flour and cook for 3 minutes, stirring constantly. Gradually pour in the milk, a little at a time, beating vigorously to prevent lumps from forming. Season with the salt, pepper, and nutmeg.

Bring to a boil and simmer for 5–10 minutes, stirring constantly. If lumps form, beat with a wire whisk until smooth.

Melt the remaining butter in a large saucepan over low heat. Stir in the white and wild mushrooms and simmer for 10 minutes, stirring often.

Add the garlic, parsley, and sherry. Season with the salt and pepper. Simmer for 3 minutes, then stir in the Béchamel sauce and half the vegetable stock. The soup should be thick and creamy. Add more stock if needed.

Cook for 3 more minutes and serve hot.

Béchamel Sauce
3 tablespoons butter
3 tablespoons all-purpose (plain) flour
3 cups (750 ml) milk
Salt and freshly ground black pepper
$1/2$ teaspoon ground nutmeg

$1/4$ cup (60 g) butter
8 oz (250 g) white mushrooms, cleaned and cut in small cubes
8 oz (250 g) wild mushrooms, cleaned and finely chopped
2 cloves garlic, finely chopped
3 tablespoons finely chopped parsley
1 cup (250 ml) dry sherry
Salt and freshly ground black pepper
$1^{1}/_{3}$ cups (330 ml) vegetable stock

Flower Soup
with potatoes and leeks

Set aside a few flowers to garnish. Finely chop the remaining flowers.

Boil the chopped flowers in the stock for 10 minutes.

Sauté the leeks in the oil in a large saucepan over medium heat until softened, about 5 minutes.

Mix in the flower stock and mashed potato. If the soup is too liquid, stir in enough of the flour and water mixture to thicken. Season with salt and pepper. Simmer for 10 minutes, stirring constantly.

Serve hot with the cubes of warm toast and the reserved flowers.

4 oz (120 g) edible flowers (daisies, cornflowers, mimosa, lilac, nasturtiums, pansies, roses)

1 quart (1 liter) boiling vegetable stock

White of 2 leeks thinly sliced

2 tablespoons extra-virgin olive oil

1 large potato, boiled and mashed

1 tablespoon all-purpose (plain) flour mixed in 3 tablespoons water (optional)

Salt and freshly ground black pepper

Cubes of toasted bread, to serve

Gazpacho
with almonds

Place the tomatoes, bell pepper, cucumber, spring onion, garlic, bread, and almonds in the bowl of a food processor and chop until smooth.

Add the oil, vinegar, and water. Season with salt and pepper. Process again for a few seconds to mix well.

Ladle into serving bowls. Garnish with a slice of bell pepper and cucumber and with cilantro and garlic, if liked. Serve at once.

- 1 lb (500 g) ripe tomatoes, peeled (from the refrigerator)
- 1 red bell pepper (capsicum), cored and coarsely chopped
- 1 cucumber, peeled and chopped
- 1 spring onion, chopped
- 8 oz (250 g) fresh bread crumbs
- 1/2 cup (75 g) almonds, toasted
- 1 clove garlic + extra to garnish (optional)
- 1/4 cup (60 ml) extra-virgin olive oil
- 2 tablespoons white wine vinegar
- Salt and freshly ground black pepper
- Fresh cilantro (coriander), to garnish

Potato Soup
with zucchini flowers

Sauté the potatoes and onion in the butter in a frying pan until lightly browned, 7–10 minutes. Add 1 cup (250 ml) of stock and simmer until it reduces.

Simmer the zucchini and zucchini flowers in a large saucepan with the oil and the remaining 1 cup (250 ml) of stock for 10 minutes. Season with the salt and pepper.

Transfer the cooked potato mixture and the zucchini mixture to a food processor or blender. Process until smooth.

Return to the saucepan and simmer for 5 minutes more. Swirl with the yogurt and garnish with the herbs, if using. Serve hot.

- 14 oz (400 g) potatoes, peeled and finely chopped
- 1 onion, finely chopped
- 2 tablespoons butter
- 2 cups (500 ml) boiling vegetable stock
- 1½ lb (750 g) zucchini (courgettes), cut in thin wheels
- 10 oz (300 g) zucchini (courgette) flowers, washed carefully and cut in half
- 2 tablespoons extra-virgin olive oil
- Salt and freshly ground black pepper
- 2 tablespoons plain yogurt
- Fresh herbs, to garnish (optional)

Onion Soup

Sauté the spring onions in the butter in a large saucepan over low heat until softened, about 5 minutes.

Heat the vegetable stock and milk in separate saucepans.

Sprinkle the spring onion mixture with the cornstarch. Gradually pour in the stock, alternating with the milk, stirring constantly. Season with salt and nutmeg.

Simmer for 20 minutes over low heat, stirring often.

Add the parsley, Parmesan, and egg yolks, beating until just blended. Simmer for 5 minutes more and serve hot.

- 8 spring onions, very thinly sliced (reserve a few rings to garnish)
- 1 tablespoon butter
- 3 cups (750 ml) vegetable stock
- 1 cup (250 ml) milk
- 1 tablespoon cornstarch (cornflour)
- Salt
- 1/2 teaspoon freshly grated nutmeg
- 1 tablespoon finely chopped parsley
- 4 tablespoons freshly grated Parmesan cheese
- 2 egg yolks, lightly beaten

Chunky Soup
with zucchini

Heat the oil in a heavy-bottomed saucepan and sauté the spring onions until softened, 3–4 minutes.

Add the zucchini and sauté for 5 more minutes. Season with salt and pepper. Add the stock and simmer over medium-low heat until the zucchini are tender, about 10 minutes.

Add the eggs, parsley, and basil and stir rapidly. Sprinkle with the Parmesan. Serve hot with croutons, if liked.

1/4 cup (60 ml) extra-virgin olive oil
2 spring onions, finely chopped
8 zucchini (courgettes(, diced
Salt and freshly ground black pepper
6 cups (1.5 liters) vegetable stock
2 eggs, lightly beaten
1 tablespoon finely chopped parsley
1 tablespoon finely chopped basil
8 tablespoons freshly grated Parmesan cheese
Croutons, to serve (optional)

PREPARATION 5 min

COOKING 20 min

DIFFICULTY level I

Bouillon
with rice and herbs

Bring the stock to a boil and add the rice. Simmer until the rice is tender, about 15 minutes.

Just before removing from the heat, add the parsley, butter, and sage. Season with salt. Serve hot with the Parmesan passed separately.

6 cups (1.5 liters) vegetable bouillon or stock

1 cup (200 g) short-grain rice

4 tablespoons finely chopped parsley

1–2 fresh sage leaves, finely chopped

Salt

1 tablespoon butter

8 tablespoons freshly grated Parmesan cheese

Garlic Soup

Place the water and garlic in a large saucepan over medium heat. Add the cloves and sage and season with salt and pepper. Bring to a boil. Simmer until the garlic is very tender, about 20 minutes.

Preheat the oven to 400°F (200°C/gas 6). Arrange the slices of baguette on an oiled baking sheet. Top each piece of bread with a little of the cheese. Drizzle with the oil and season with pepper. Bake until crisp and lightly browned, 5–7 minutes.

Purée the soup in a blender until smooth and creamy.

Arrange the crostini in serving bowls and then ladle the soup over the top. Serve hot.

6 cups (1.5 liters) water
30 cloves garlic, peeled
2 cloves
3 sage leaves
Salt and freshly ground black pepper
1 large baguette (French loaf), sliced
6 oz (180 g) Gruyère cheese,
    coarsely grated
1/4 cup (60 ml) extra-virgin olive oil

Mexican Gazpacho

Cut the avocado in half lengthwise and twist each half so that the large pit breaks free from the flesh. Remove the rind and scrape out the flesh.

Mix the avocado flesh with the lime juice in a medium bowl.

Process the avocado mixture, tomatoes, cucumber, bell pepper, spring onions, garlic, parsley, basil, oil, and water in a food processor or blender until smooth. Season with salt and pepper. Refrigerate for 2 hours.

Serve chilled.

1 firm-ripe avocado
Freshly squeezed juice of 1 lime
3 large firm-ripe tomatoes, peeled and finely chopped
1 medium cucumber, peeled and finely chopped
1 green bell pepper (capsicum), seeded and finely chopped
4 spring onions, finely chopped
1 clove garlic, finely chopped
1 bunch parsley, finely chopped
6 leaves fresh basil, torn
2 tablespoons extra-virgin olive oil
2 cups (500 ml) water
Salt and freshly ground white pepper

Red Lentil Soup
with mango

Place the lentils in a large pot of cold water and bring to a boil. Simmer until tender, 30–35 minutes. Drain and set aside.

Heat the oil over low heat in the same pot. Add the onion, garlic, and mango and sauté until softened, about 5 minutes.

Add the lentils and potatoes and pour in the stock. Bring to a boil and simmer over low heat for 30 minutes.

Stir in the tomatoes, cumin, chile, paprika, and thyme. Season with salt and pepper. Simmer for 10 minutes.

Stir in the lemon juice. Remove from the heat and blend with a handheld blender until partially smooth. Return to the heat and reheat gently. Serve hot with the toast.

1 cup (100 g) red lentils, rinsed
1 tablespoon extra-virgin olive oil
1/2 onion, finely sliced
2 cloves garlic, finely chopped
3 tablespoons chopped dried mango
2 potatoes, peeled and diced
3 cups (750 ml) chicken stock
    (homemade or bouillon cube)
1 (14-oz/400-g) can tomatoes, with juice
1/2 teaspoon ground cumin
1/2 teaspoon ground red chile
1/2 teaspoon sweet paprika
1/2 teaspoon dried thyme
Salt and freshly ground black pepper
2 tablespoons fresh lemon juice
Warm toast, buttered, to serve

Vegetable Cream

Heat the butter in a large saucepan over medium heat. Add the onion, celery, carrot, red pepper flakes, and caraway seeds and sauté until the vegetables are softened, about 10 minutes.

Add the bay leaf, parsley, garlic, dill, and cabbage. Sauté until the cabbage is wilted and half its original bulk, about 5 minutes. Add the potatoes, turnips, salt, pepper, and stock. Bring to a boil, cover, and simmer for 30 minutes.

 Add the tomatoes. Partially cover the pan and simmer on low heat for 30 minutes.

Discard the bay leaf. Purée the soup in a blender in two batches until free of lumps, but still with a bit of texture. Taste for salt and pepper. Serve hot with a dollop of sour cream and a sprig of fresh dill.

2 tablespoons butter
1 large onion, chopped
2 large stalks celery, chopped
1 large carrot, chopped
Pinch of red pepper flakes
1 teaspoon caraway seeds
1 bay leaf
2 tablespoons finely chopped parsley
3 cloves garlic, finely chopped
Handful of chopped fresh dill
1 lb (500 g) cabbage, chopped
2 lb (1 kg) potatoes, peeled and cut into cubes
1 lb (500 g) turnips, peeled and coarsely chopped
1 teaspoon salt
1 teaspoon freshly ground black pepper
6 cups (1.5 liters) vegetable stock (homemade or bouillon cube)
1 (14-oz/400-g) can tomatoes, with juice
Sour cream, to garnish
Few sprigs of fresh dill, to garnish

Cabbage Soup

SERVES 4

PREPARATION 15 min

COOKING 1 h

DIFFICULTY level 1

Sauté the garlic in the oil in a large saucepan over low heat until pale gold, 2–3 minutes. Add the cabbage and sauté until wilted.

Pour in the vegetable stock and simmer for 40 minutes. Season with the salt and pepper.

Preheat the oven to 350°F (180°C/gas 4).

Place a layer of toasted bread in a Dutch oven or casserole. Sprinkle with the Parmesan and pour in 1½ cups (375 ml) of the soup. Repeat until all the ingredients are in the pot.

Bake for 10 minutes and serve hot.

- 3 cloves garlic, finely chopped
- 2 tablespoons extra-virgin olive oil
- 1¾ lb (800 g) Savoy cabbage, shredded
- 1 quart (1 liter) vegetable stock
- Salt and freshly ground black pepper
- 4–8 slices of day-old firm-textured bread, toasted
- 8 tablespoons freshly grated Parmesan cheese

Minestrone

with lentils and beans

Bring 8 cups (2 liters) of water to a boil in a large saucepan with the garbanzo beans and lentils. Skim off any foam. Reduce the heat and simmer until the beans are almost tender, about 1 hour. Drain, reserving the stock.

Sauté the onion in the oil in a large saucepan over low heat for 5 minutes. Add the herbs and tomatoes and simmer for 3 minutes.

Add the remaining 8 cups (2 liters) of water and bring to a boil. Season with salt and add all the vegetables. Simmer over medium-low heat for 30 minutes.

Add the drained beans and lentils and about half of the reserved stock. Add the garlic and butter to the pot. Simmer until the vegetables are tender, 30–45 minutes.

Cook the pasta in the boiling soup until al dente. If there is not enough liquid, add more of the reserved stock as needed.

Sprinkle with pecorino and season with black pepper. Serve hot.

4 quarts (4 liters) water

1 cup (150 g) dried garbanzo beans (chickpeas), soaked overnight

1 cup (150 g) lentils

1/4 cup (60 ml) extra-virgin olive oil

1 onion, finely chopped

3 tablespoons finely chopped mixed fresh herbs (such as marjoram, thyme, parsley, and sage)

1 cup (250 ml) tomato passata (sieved tomatoes)

Salt

1 lb (500 g) mixed vegetables (carrots, celery, spinach, Swiss chard, potatoes, zucchini (courgettes), finely chopped

2 cloves garlic

1/4 cup (30 g) butter, cut up

8 oz (250 g) small soup pasta

1/4 cup (30 g) freshly grated pecorino cheese

Freshly ground black pepper

SERVES 4–6

PREPARATION 20 min + time to soak beans

COOKING 1 h 30 min

DIFFICULTY level 1

Bean Soup
with croutons

Soak the garbanzo, borlotti, and cannellini beans in cold water for 12 hours. Drain well and cook for about 1 hour, or until the beans are all tender. Drain.

Cook the lentils in a pan of salted, boiling water for about 30 minutes, or until tender. Drain and set aside.

Cook the spelt in a pan of salted, boiling water for the time indicated on the package, or until tender. Drain and set aside.

Sauté the onion, carrot, celery, parsley, and sage in the oil in a large frying pan over medium heat until softened, about 5 minutes. Season with salt and pepper.

Add the tomatoes, beans, lentils, spelt, and vegetable stock, and simmer for 10 minutes. Garnish with the croutons and serve hot.

$1/2$ cup (50 g) garbanzo beans (chickpeas)

$1/2$ cup (50 g) dried borlotti beans

$1/2$ cup (50 g) dried cannellini beans

$1/2$ cup (50 g) lentils

$1/2$ cup (50 g) spelt or pearl barley

1 onion, 1 carrot, 1 stalk celery, 4 leaves basil, 1 sprig parsley, and 1 leaf sage, finely chopped

$1/2$ cup (125 ml) extra-virgin olive oil

1 cup (250 g) peeled and chopped tomatoes

1 quart (1 liter) vegetable stock

Salt and freshly ground black pepper

10 oz (300 g) croutons

SAVORY PIES, FOCACCIA, & PIZZA

MAKES one (12-inch/30-cm) pizza
PREPARATION 20 min
RISING TIME 1 h 30 min
COOKING 20–25 min
DIFFICULTY level 1

Basic Pizza Dough

Prepare the yeast and dough following the instructions on these pages.

Preheat the oven to 425°F (220°C/gas 7). Oil a pizza pan or baking sheet.

When the rising time has elapsed (about 1 hour 30 minutes), transfer the dough to a lightly floured work surface and knead for 2–3 minutes.

Place the dough in the prepared pan or baking sheet and use your fingertips to spread into a disk about 12 inches (30 cm) in diameter and $\frac{1}{2}$ inch (1 cm) thick. Dimple the surface with your fingertips.

Drizzle with the remaining oil, if making focaccia, or spread with the topping, if making pizza. Bake according to the instructions in the recipes.

- 1 oz (30 g) fresh yeast or 2 ($\frac{1}{4}$-oz/7-g) packages active dry yeast
- 1 teaspoon sugar
- About 1 cup (250 ml) warm water
- 3$\frac{1}{3}$ cups (500 g) all-purpose (plain) flour
- 1 teaspoon salt
- $\frac{1}{4}$ cup (60 ml) extra-virgin olive oil

The dough

1 Place the flour and salt in a large bowl. Pour in the yeast mixture, most of the remaining water, and any other ingredients listed in the recipe. Stir until the flour is absorbed, adding more water as required.

2 Sprinkle a work surface with a little flour (note that flour used to prepare the work surface is

1

The yeast

To prepare the yeast you will need a small bowl, a fork, warm water, and sugar. Exact quantities are given in each recipe.

1 Put the fresh or active dry yeast in the bowl. If using fresh yeast, crumble it into the bowl.

2 Add the sugar and half the warm water and stir with a fork until the yeast has dissolved.

3 Set the mixture aside for about 10 minutes. It will look creamy when ready. Stir again before proceeding to make the dough.

1

2

3

not included in the quantities given in the recipes. Allow about $1/2$ cup (75 g extra). Transfer the dough to the work surface. Shape into a compact ball.

3 Press down on the dough with your knuckles to spread it. Take the far end of the dough, fold it a short distance toward you, then push it away again with the heel

of your palm. Flexing your wrist, fold it toward you again, give it a quarter turn, then push it away. Repeat, gently and with the lightest possible touch, for 8–10 minutes. When ready, the dough should be smooth and elastic, show definite air bubbles beneath the surface, and spring back if you flatten it with your palm.

4 Place in a large bowl and cover with a cloth. It should double in volume during rising. To test, poke your finger gently into the dough; if the impression remains, it is ready. The rising times given are approximate; yeast is a living ingredient affected by temperature and humidity, among other things. Some days it will take longer to rise than others.

2

3

4

SERVES 4

PREPARATION 30 min

RISING TIME 1 h 30 min

COOKING 20–25 min

DIFFICULTY level 2

Vegetable Pizza
with whole-wheat base

Base: Mix the yeast, 1/2 cup (125 ml) of the water, and sugar in a small bowl. Set aside until foamy, about 10 minutes.

Sift the three flours and salt into a large bowl and make a well in the center. Stir in the yeast mixture and as much of the remaining water as required to obtain a firm dough.

Knead until smooth and elastic, 8–10 minutes. Shape into a ball, place in an oiled bowl, and cover with a clean cloth. Let rise in a warm place for 45 minutes.

Turn out onto a lightly floured work surface and knead for 10 minutes. Return to the bowl, cover with a clean cloth, and let rise until doubled in bulk, about 45 minutes.

Preheat the oven to 375°F (190°C/gas 5). Oil a 13-inch (32-cm) pizza pan.

Topping: Sauté the eggplant, garlic, and parsley in 1/4 cup (60 ml) of oil in a frying pan over medium heat until the eggplant is lightly browned. Add the zucchini and sauté for 5 minutes.

Place the risen pizza dough in the prepared pan, pushing it outward with your fingertips to cover the bottom of the pan in an even layer. Sprinkle the vegetable mixture, olives, pecorino, and tomatoes on top. Drizzle with the remaining oil.

Bake until the dough is cooked and the vegetables are tender, 25–30 minutes. Serve hot or at room temperature.

Base

- 1 oz (30 g) fresh yeast or 2 packages (1/4 oz/7 g) active dry yeast
- 1 1/3 cups (300 ml) warm water + more as needed
- 1 teaspoon sugar
- 2 cups (300 g) unbleached flour
- 1 cup (150 g) all-purpose (plain) flour
- 1 cup (150 g) whole-wheat (wholemeal) flour
- 1 teaspoon salt

Topping

- 1 eggplant (aubergine), cut in small cubes
- 1 clove garlic, finely chopped
- 1 tablespoon finely chopped parsley
- 1/3 cup (90 ml) extra-virgin olive oil
- 5 oz (150 g) zucchini (courgettes), cut in small cubes
- 20 green olives, pitted
- 5 oz (150 g) pecorino cheese, cut into small cubes
- 12 cherry tomatoes, cut in half

SERVES 2–4
PREPARATION 40 min
RISING TIME 1 h 30 min
COOKING 30–35 min
DIFFICULTY level 1

Onion Pizza
with bell peppers

Prepare the pizza dough and set aside to rise.

Preheat the oven to 425°F (220°C/gas 7). Oil a 12-inch (30-cm) pizza pan.

Heat 3 tablespoons of oil in a large frying pan over medium heat. Add the onions and sauté until transparent, 3–4 minutes. Add the bell peppers and sauté until softened, 7–10 minutes. Season with salt and pepper.

Knead the risen pizza dough briefly on a lightly floured work surface then press it into the prepared pan using your hands.

Spread the dough with the onion and bell pepper mixture. Top with the sundried tomatoes. Sprinkle with the olives and drizzle with the remaining oil.

Bake until the base is crisp and golden brown, about 20 minutes.

Garnish with the basil. Serve hot or at room temperature.

1 quantity pizza dough (see pages 72–73)
¹⁄₄ cup (60 ml) extra-virgin olive oil
2 large onions, finely sliced
2 large red bell peppers (capsicums), seeded and thinly sliced
Salt and freshly ground black pepper
4–6 sundried tomatoes, chopped
¹⁄₄ cup (50 g) black olives, pitted
Fresh basil leaves, to garnish

Onion Pizza
with cheese and walnuts

Prepare the pizza dough and set aside to rise.

Preheat the oven to 425°F (220°C/gas 7). Oil a 12-inch (30-cm) pizza pan.

Beat the Gorgonzola in a bowl with a fork, until smooth and creamy. Stir in the Worcestershire sauce.

Knead the risen dough briefly on a lightly floured work surface then press it into the prepared pan using your hands. Spread with the Gorgonzola and top with the onions. Sprinkle with the walnuts.

Bake for 15 minutes. Dot with the cream cheese and season with salt and pepper. Bake until the base is crisp and golden brown, 5–10 minutes.

Serve hot or at room temperature.

1 quantity pizza dough (see pages 72–73)
8 oz (250 g) Gorgonzola cheese, at room temperature
1 tablespoon Worcestershire sauce
1 large white onion, thinly sliced
²⁄₃ cup (100 g) walnuts
3 oz (90 g) cream cheese
Salt and freshly ground black pepper

SERVES 2–4
PREPARATION 30 min
RISING TIME 1 h 30 min
COOKING 20 min
DIFFICULTY level 1

Tomato Pizza
with oregano

Prepare the pizza dough, incorporating the mashed potato and 2 tablespoons of oil into the dough as you knead. Set aside to rise.

Preheat the oven to 425°F (220°C/gas 7). Oil a 12-inch (30-cm) pizza pan.

Knead the risen dough briefly on a lightly floured work surface then press it into the prepared pan using your hands. Place the tomatoes on the dough. Season with salt, pepper, and oregano. Drizzle with the remaining oil.

Bake until the base is crisp and golden brown, about 20 minutes.

Serve hot or at room temperature.

1 quantity pizza dough (see pages 72–73)
1 large potato, boiled and mashed
1/4 cup (60 ml) extra-virgin olive oil
Salt and freshly ground black pepper
20 cherry tomatoes, thinly sliced
1 teaspoon dried oregano

SERVES 4

PREPARATION 40 min

COOKING 1 h

DIFFICULTY level 2

Goat Cheese
and vegetable puff

Preheat the oven to 375°F (190°C/gas 5). Oil a 10-inch (25-cm) pie pan.

Grill the eggplants in a grill pan until tender. Broil (grill) the bell peppers whole in the oven until the skins are blackened all over. Wrap in aluminum foil for 10 minutes, then remove the skins. Slice into long strips. Rinse carefully and dry well.

Place the goat cheese in a large bowl with the egg, egg yolks, garlic, and salt and pepper. Mix well with a wooden spoon.

Roll the pastry out on a lightly floured work surface to fit the bottom and sides of the pan. Prick all over with a fork.

Spoon the goat cheese filling into the pastry. Arrange the tomatoes, bell peppers, and eggplant on top. Sprinkle with basil or mint, if liked, and season with salt and pepper.

Bake until the pastry is golden brown, 30–35 minutes. Serve hot or at room temperature.

8 oz (250 g) eggplants (aubergines), thinly sliced

2 red bell peppers (capsicums), seeded, cored, and halved

1¼ cups (310 g) fresh creamy goat cheese

1 egg and 2 egg yolks

1 clove garlic, finely chopped

Salt and freshly ground black pepper

8 oz (250 g) frozen puff pastry, thawed

10 cherry tomatoes, sliced

6 leaves fresh basil or mint, torn (optional)

Tomato Quiche

Pastry: Sift the flour and salt into a large bowl and cut in the butter with a pastry cutter (or rub in with your finger tips), until the mixture resembles bread crumbs. Gradually stir in enough water to make a smooth dough. Shape into a ball and wrap in plastic wrap (cling film). Refrigerate for 1 hour.

Preheat the oven to 350°F (180°C/gas 4). Butter a 10-inch (25-cm) pie pan or springform pan.

Filling: Cut the cherry tomatoes in half and gently squeeze out as many seeds as possible.

Beat the eggs, cream, ricotta, Parmesan, salt, and pepper in a medium bowl with an electric mixer at medium speed until well mixed. Stir in the basil and oregano.

Roll out the pastry on a lightly floured work surface to ¼-inch (5 mm) thick. Line the prepared pan with the pastry.

Pour the egg and cheese mixture over the base. Add the tomatoes one by one, cut side down, pressing them into the filling slightly.

Bake until golden brown and set, about 45 minutes.

Serve hot or at room temperature.

Pastry
2 cups (300 g) all-purpose (plain) flour
¼ teaspoon salt
1 cup (250 g) butter, cut up
⅓ cup (90 ml) water

Filling
15–20 cherry tomatoes
4 large eggs
½ cup (125 ml) heavy (double) cream
½ cup (125 g) fresh ricotta cheese, drained
6 tablespoons freshly grated Parmesan cheese
Salt and freshly ground black pepper
4–6 leaves fresh basil, finely chopped
½ teaspoon dried oregano

SERVES 4

PREPARATION 30 min + time to make pastry

COOKING 30–35 min

DIFFICULTY level 2

Fava Bean Quiche

Prepare the pastry and chill in the refrigerator.

Preheat the oven to 400°F (200°C/gas 6). Set out a 10-inch (26-cm) pie pan.

Coarsely chop a third of the fava beans. Process the remaining fava beans in a food processor or blender with the ricotta, cream, Parmesan, Tabasco, salt and pepper until well blended.

Roll the dough out and use it to line the pan, letting it overlap the edges. Prick with a fork.

Spoon in half the chopped fava beans, the filling, and top with the remaining fava beans. Fold in the overlapping edges. Brush with the beaten egg.

Bake until golden, 30–35 minutes. Serve warm.

1 quantity pastry (see page 82)
10 oz (300 g) fava (broad) beans, lightly boiled
1¼ cups (300 g) ricotta cheese, drained
¾ cup (180 ml) single (light) cream
¾ cup (90 g) freshly grated Parmesan cheese
2 drops Tabasco sauce
Salt and freshly ground black pepper
1 egg, lightly beaten

Ratatouille Quiche

Sprinkle the eggplant with coarse sea salt and let rest for 1 hour.

Preheat the oven to 350°F (180°C/gas 4). Grease a 10-inch (25-cm) quiche or pie pan.

Roll out the pastry on a lightly floured work surface ¼-inch (5-mm) thick. Line the base and sides of the pan with the pastry. Bake until risen and golden brown, about 15 minutes.

Rinse and drain the eggplant. Chop coarsely.

Heat the oil in a large frying pan over medium heat. Add the onions, garlic, eggplant, zucchini, and bell peppers and sauté until softened, 5–7 minutes. Add the tomatoes, bay leaf, and thyme. Mix well and simmer until tender, 10–15 minutes. Season with salt and pepper.

Spoon the ratatouille into the pastry case. Top with mozzarella and sprinkle with parsley and basil. Serve hot.

2 large eggplants (aubergines), cut in small cubes

Coarse sea salt

10 oz (300 g) frozen puff pastry, thawed

¼ cup (60 ml) extra-virgin olive oil

2 medium onions, chopped

2 cloves garlic, finely chopped

3 zucchini (courgettes), sliced

3 green bell peppers, (capsicums) seeded and sliced

1 lb (500 g) tomatoes, peeled and chopped

1 bay leaf

Leaves from sprig of thyme

Salt and freshly ground black pepper

4 oz (125 g) fresh mozzarella pieces

2 tablespoons finely chopped parsley

1 tablespoon finely chopped basil

Vegetable Pie

Preheat the oven to 375°F (190°C/gas 5). Oil a 10-inch (28-cm) pie pan.

Sauté the onion in the oil in a large frying pan over medium heat until softened, 3–4 minutes. Add the bell peppers, zucchini, and eggplants and sauté over low heat for 5 minutes. Add the tomatoes and season with salt. Cover and simmer over very low heat for 15 minutes, stirring occasionally, adding the stock if the mixture dries out.

Roll the pastry out to 1/8-inch (3-mm) thick. Line the base and sides of the prepared pan with the pastry. Prick all over with a fork. Cover with pie weights or dried beans. Bake until lightly browned, 15–18 minutes. Discard the paper and beans.

Mix the vegetables, ricotta, Parmesan, and egg yolk in a large bowl. Fill the pastry case with the vegetable mixture.

Bake until the filling has set, 20–25 minutes. Serve hot or at room temperature.

1/2 onion

3 tablespoons extra-virgin olive oil

1/2 yellow bell pepper (capsicum), seeded, cored, and chopped

1/2 red bell pepper (capsicum), seeded, cored, and chopped

1 small zucchini (courgette), cut into sticks

4 oz (125 g) eggplant (aubergines), diced

10 cherry tomatoes, diced

Salt

1/4 cup (60 ml) vegetable stock

8 oz (250 g) frozen puff pastry, thawed

2/3 cup (150 g) ricotta cheese, drained

4 tablespoons freshly grated Parmesan cheese

1 egg yolk

Zucchini Quiche

Preheat the oven to 400°F (200°C/gas 6). Butter a 10-inch (25-cm) pie plate or springform pan.

Place the pastry on a lightly floured work surface and sprinkle with 1 tablespoon of poppy seeds. Roll out into a thin sheet. Line the prepared pan with the pastry. Cover with a sheet of waxed paper and fill with pie weights or dried beans. Bake blind for 20 minutes.

Trim the zucchini flowers and cut each one into 3–4 pieces. Slice the zucchini thinly lengthwise. Sauté the zucchini in the butter in a large frying pan over medium heat for 3 minutes. Add the flowers and sauté for 5 minutes.

Beat the eggs and egg yolk in a medium bowl with an electric mixer at high speed until frothy. Season with salt and pepper. Add the arugula, cream, and Parmesan. Mix in the sautéed zucchini and flowers.

Pour the mixture into the pastry case and sprinkle with the remaining poppy seeds.

Bake until golden brown and set, about 25 minutes. Serve hot or at room temperature.

8 oz (250 g) frozen puff pastry, thawed
2 tablespoons poppy seeds
6 zucchini (courgettes), with flowers attached
2 tablespoons butter
2 eggs + 1 egg yolk
 Salt and freshly ground black pepper
1 bunch arugula (rocket), shredded
2/3 cup (180 ml) heavy (double) cream
8 tablespoons freshly grated Parmesan cheese

SERVES 4–6
PREPARATION 30 min
RISING TIME 2 h
COOKING 20–25 min
DIFFICULTY level 2

Herb Focaccia

Prepare the pizza dough. Gradually work 2 tablespoons of the oil into the dough as you knead. Let rise in a warm place until doubled in volume, about 2 hours.

Preheat the oven to 450°F (250°C/gas 8).

Turn the dough out onto a lightly floured work surface and knead for 5 minutes. Press the dough into an oiled 8 x12-inch (20 x 30-cm) baking pan using your fingertips.

Mix together the onion, garlic, parsley, basil, rosemary, and oregano in a small bowl. Add 2 tablespoons of the remaining oil and season with pepper. Spread the tomatoes over the focaccia and top with the herb mixture. Season with salt and drizzle with the remaining oil.

Bake until the focaccia is golden brown, 20–25 minutes. Serve hot or at room temperature.

1 quantity pizza dough (see pages 72–73)
$1/3$ cup (90 ml) extra-virgin olive oil
1 medium onion, very finely chopped
2 cloves garlic, very finely chopped
3 tablespoons finely chopped parsley
2 tablespoons finely chopped basil
1 tablespoon finely chopped rosemary
$1/2$ teaspoon dried oregano
Salt and freshly ground black pepper
1 (14-oz/400-g) can tomatoes,
   with juice, chopped

SERVES 4
PREPARATION 30 min
RISING TIME 1 h 30 min
COOKING 25 min
DIFFICULTY level 1

Focaccia
with tomatoes and pecorino

Prepare the pizza dough and set aside to rise.

Slice the tomatoes and place in a colander. Sprinkle with salt and let drain for 10 minutes.

Preheat the oven to 450°F (250°C/gas 8). Oil a baking sheet.

Roll out the dough on a lightly floured work surface into a 12-inch (30-cm) disk. Transfer the dough to the prepared baking sheet. Dimple the surface with your fingertips.

Bake until pale golden brown, about 20 minutes. Remove from the oven and cover with the tomatoes and mozzarella. Season with salt and pepper. Sprinkle with oregano and basil and drizzle with the oil. Bake for 5 minutes more.

Sprinkle with the pecorino and serve hot or at room temperature.

1 quantity pizza dough (see pages 72–73)
2 tablespoons extra-virgin olive oil
10–12 cherry tomatoes
Salt and freshly ground black pepper
8 oz (250 g) mozzarella cheese, thinly sliced
1/2 teaspoon dried oregano
8 leaves fresh basil, torn
1/2 cup (60 g) aged pecorino cheese, thinly sliced

PASTA & GNOCCHI

SERVES 4–6

PREPARATION 10 min

COOKING 15 min

DIFFICULTY level 1

Spaghetti
with tomato and lemon

Blanch the tomatoes in boiling water for 2 minutes. Drain and peel them. Chop coarsely.

Cook the pasta in a large pot of salted boiling water until al dente. Drain well and transfer to a large serving dish.

Add the tomatoes, basil, oil, lemon juice, and garlic. Season with salt and pepper. Toss well. Garnish with basil and serve hot.

2 lb (1 kg) ripe tomatoes
1 lb (500 g) spaghetti
4 tablespoons finely chopped basil
    + extra leaves, to garnish
1/3 cup (90 ml) extra-virgin olive oil
Freshly squeezed juice of 1 lemon
2 cloves garlic, finely chopped
Salt and freshly ground black pepper

SERVES 4–6

PREPARATION 15 min

COOKING 20 min

DIFFICULTY level 2

Linguine
with pesto, potatoes, and beans

Bring a large pot of salted water to a boil over high heat. Cook the green beans in a pot of salted boiling water until almost tender, 3–4 minutes. Drain, reserving the cooking water, and set aside.

Return the boiling water to the heat and cook the linguine for 5 minutes. Add the potatoes and cook until the pasta is al dente and the potatoes are tender, about 7–8 minutes more.

Drain well, reserving 3 tablespoons of the cooking liquid, and transfer to a large serving bowl. Add the oil and reserved cooking liquid to the pesto.

Spoon over the pasta and potatoes, add the green beans and toss well. Season with pepper. Sprinkle with the Parmesan. Garnish with basil and serve hot.

14 oz (400 g) green beans, chopped
1 lb (500 g) linguine
6–8 new potatoes, cut into small cubes
3 tablespoons extra-virgin olive oil
1 quantity pesto (see page 118)
Freshly ground black pepper
1 oz (30 g) Parmesan, cut into flakes
Sprigs of basil, to garnish

Bucatini
with tomato and almonds

Sweat the onion in a frying pan with 1 tablespoon of oil for 10 minutes. Add the tomatoes and season with salt and pepper. Cover and simmer over low heat for 20–25 minutes.

Toast the almonds in a small frying pan over low heat. Remove from the heat and chop coarsely.

Sauté the bread in a frying pan with the remaining oil until crisp and brown, about 5 minutes.

Cook the bucatini in plenty of salted, boiling water until al dente. Drain and transfer to a heated serving bowl. Pour the sauce over the top. Sprinkle with the almonds, bread, and pecorino. Toss well and serve hot.

1 medium onion, finely chopped

1/4 cup (60 ml) extra-virgin olive oil

1 lb (500 g) canned tomatoes, with juice, coarsely chopped

Salt and freshly ground black pepper

3 oz (90 g) almonds

4 thick slices day-old firm-textured bread, cut in cubes

1 lb (500 g) bucatini

3/4 cup (75 g) freshly grated pecorino cheese

Linguine
with dried tomatoes and capers

Cut the fresh tomatoes in half or in quarters and squeeze them gently to remove the seeds. Sprinkle lightly with salt and leave to drain for 10 minutes.

Heat the oil in a heavy-bottomed saucepan over low heat. Add the dried tomatoes and cook over low heat for a few minutes before adding the fresh tomatoes, capers, garlic, and red pepper flakes. Season with salt. Simmer for 20 minutes.

Cook the linguine in a large pan of salted, boiling water until al dente.

Drain and place in a heated serving dish. Toss well with the sauce and serve hot.

2 lb (1 kg) tomatoes, peeled
Salt
4 oz (125 g) dried tomatoes, finely chopped
4 tablespoons salt-cured capers
1 clove garlic, peeled but whole
1/3 cup (90 ml) extra-virgin olive oil
1/2 teaspoon red pepper flakes
1 lb (500 g) linguine

Spaghetti
with summer vegetables

Bring a large pot of salted water to a boil over high heat. Cook the green beans in the water until tender, about 7 minutes. Drain well, reserving the cooking water.

Return the water to the heat and bring to a boil. Cook the pasta in the water until al dente. Drain well.

Transfer the pasta to a serving bowl and add 2 tablespoons of the oil. Toss well. Add the garlic, green beans, celery, tomatoes, zucchini, bell pepper, arugula, the remaining oil, and the vinegar. Season with salt and pepper, and toss well.

Serve immediately.

- 5 oz (150 g) green beans, trimmed and cut in short lengths
- 1 lb (500 g) whole-wheat (wholemeal) spaghetti
- 1/3 cup (90 ml) extra-virgin olive oil
- 1 clove garlic, finely chopped
- 2 celery sticks, chopped
- 20 cherry tomatoes, quartered
- 3 small zucchini (courgettes), cut into julienne strips
- 1 yellow bell pepper (capsicum), seeded and cut into small squares
- 3 oz (90 g) arugula (rocket), chopped
- 1 tablespoon white wine vinegar
- Salt and freshly ground black pepper

Spicy Farfalle
with yogurt sauce and avocado

Sauté the garlic and onion in 2 tablespoons of oil in a frying pan over medium heat until pale gold, about 5 minutes Add the wine and simmer until evaporated.

Cook the pasta in a large pot of salted, boiling water until al dente.

Peel, pit, and dice the avocado. Drizzle with the lemon juice to prevent it from browning.

Beat the yogurt with the remaining oil in a large bowl. Season with salt and pepper. Add the chile pepper, celery, capers, and parsley.

Drain the pasta and toss in the yogurt sauce. Add the onion and avocado, toss again, and serve.

2 cloves garlic, finely chopped
1 large onion, chopped
$\frac{1}{4}$ cup (60 ml) extra-virgin olive oil
1 tablespoon dry white wine
1 lb (500 g) farfalle
1 ripe avocado
Freshly squeezed juice of 1 lemon
1 cup (250 ml) plain yogurt
Salt and freshly ground black pepper
1 red hot chile pepper, thinly sliced
1 celery heart, thinly sliced
$1\frac{1}{2}$ tablespoons salt-cured capers, rinsed
1 tablespoon finely chopped parsley

SERVES 4–6

PREPARATION 10 min

COOKING 20 min

DIFFICULTY level 1

Tofu Penne

Simmer the tofu in a saucepan of boiling water for 4 minutes. Drain and process in a food processor or blender with the basil, parsley, almonds, oil, garlic, and salt until smooth.

Cook the pasta in a large pot of salted, boiling water until al dente. Drain well and toss gently with the sauce.

Serve hot.

5 oz (150 g) tofu (bean curd)
1 small bunch basil
1 small bunch parsley
1/3 cup (50 g) blanched almonds
1/3 cup (90 ml) extra-virgin olive oil
2 cloves garlic
Salt
1 lb (500 g) whole-wheat penne

Spicy Fusilli

Cook the Swiss chard in a large saucepan of lightly salted water over medium heat until tender, 3–5 minutes. Drain well and place in a bowl of cold water. Drain again, squeezing to remove excess moisture.

Melt the butter in a large frying pan over medium heat. Add the garlic and sauté until pale golden brown, 2–3 minutes. Add the pine nuts and bread crumbs and sauté until golden brown and crisp, about 5 minutes.

Add the Swiss chard and the golden raisins. Mix well and sauté for 2 minutes. Season with salt.

Cook the pasta in a large pan of salted, boiling water until al dente. Drain well and add to the pan with the Swiss chard mixture. Add the chile pepper and toss over high heat for 2 minutes.

Serve hot.

1½ lb (750 g) Swiss chard (silver beet), shredded

Salt

⅓ cup (60 g) pine nuts

¼ cup (60 g) butter

2 cloves garlic, finely sliced

Scant 1½ cups (80 g) fresh bread crumbs

Scant ¼ cup (30 g) golden raisins (sultanas)

1 lb (500 g) whole-wheat (wholemeal) or plain fusilli

1 small red chile pepper, seeded and sliced

Penne

with ricotta and pine nuts

Cook the pasta in a large pot of salted boiling water until al dente.

Toast the pine nuts in a large frying pan over medium heat until lightly browned, about 3 minutes. Add the butter and let it melt.

Drain the pasta and add to the frying pan. Toss well for 1–2 minutes then remove from the heat. Add the Parmesan and season with pepper.

Toss well and place in a serving dish. Arrange the ricotta on top. Sprinkle with chives and serve hot.

1 lb (500 g) whole-wheat (wholemeal) or plain penne

1/4 cup (45 g) pine nuts

1/3 cup (90 g) butter

1/2 cup (60 g) freshly grated Parmesan cheese

Freshly ground white pepper

5 oz (150 g) ricotta salata (or aged pecorino) cheese, broken into bite-size pieces

2 tablespoons finely chopped chives

Penne

with asparagus and pine nuts

Cook the asparagus in salted boiling water until tender, 5–8 minutes. Drain well and chop.

Toast the pine nuts in a large frying pan over medium heat until lightly browned, about 3 minutes. Add the oil, garlic, and tomatoes. Season with salt and pepper. Simmer over low heat until the tomatoes begin to break down, about 15 minutes.

Beat the egg with 1 tablespoon of the pecorino in a small bowl. Season with salt and pepper.

Cook the pasta in a large pan of salted, boiling water until al dente. Drain well and return to the pan. Add the egg mixture and simmer over low heat until the egg cooks, about 2 minutes. Add the tomato mixture and asparagus. Toss well. Sprinkle with pecorino and serve hot.

1 lb (500 g) asparagus spears, tough stalks removed

¼ cup (45 g) pine nuts

3 tablespoons extra-virgin olive oil

1 clove garlic, finely chopped

1 lb (500 g) ripe tomatoes, chopped

Salt and freshly ground black pepper

1 large egg

½ cup (60 g) freshly grated pecorino or Parmesan cheese

1 lb (500 g) whole-wheat (wholemeal) or plain penne

SERVES 4–6

PREPARATION 20 min

COOKING 30 min

DIFFICULTY level 2

Maltagliati
with tomatoes and yogurt

Preheat the oven to 400°F (200°C/gas 6). Place the cherry tomatoes cut side up in an ovenproof baking dish. Sprinkle with half the Parmesan, salt, pepper, and thyme. Drizzle with half the oil. Bake until the cheese is browned, 15–20 minutes.

Sauté the spring onions in the remaining oil in a large frying pan over low heat for about 7 minutes. Stir in the yogurt and remaining Parmesan. Season with salt and pepper and keep the sauce warm over very low heat.

Cook the pasta in a large pot of salted boiling water until al dente. Drain the pasta and add to the pan with the yogurt sauce. Toss gently.

Transfer to a heated serving dish, add the baked cherry tomatoes and toss again. Top with a grinding of pepper and serve hot.

- 14 oz (400 g) cherry tomatoes, cut in half
- ½ cup (75 g) freshly grated Parmesan cheese
- 2 tablespoons chopped thyme
- Salt and freshly ground black pepper
- ⅓ cup (90 ml) extra-virgin olive oil
- 14 oz (400 g) spring onions, cleaned and sliced in thin wheels
- 14 oz (400 g) quantity fresh maltagliati pasta (or use coarsely chopped fresh lasagne sheets)
- 1 cup (250 ml) plain yogurt

SERVES 4

PREPARATION 30 min

COOKING 20 min

DIFFICULTY level 2

Tagliatelle
with pesto and pine nuts

Toast the pine nuts in a small, nonstick frying pan until golden brown.

Sauté the onion in the oil in a saucepan over medium heat until softened, about 5 minutes. Stir in the tomatoes and pine nuts and cook over high heat for 5 minutes.

Cook the pasta in a large pot of salted boiling water until al dente.

Drain the pasta and add to the pan with the sauce, adding a little of the cooking water from the pasta. Add the pesto, toss gently, and serve hot.

4 tablespoons pine nuts

1 onion, finely chopped

1/3 cup (90 ml) extra-virgin olive oil

1 lb (500 g) tomatoes, peeled and coarsely chopped

14 oz (400 g) fresh tagliatelle

1/2 cup (125 ml) pesto (see page 118)

Tagliolini
with almond and basil pesto

Chop the almonds, garlic, and a pinch of salt in a food processor until almost smooth. Add the basil and tomato and chop until smooth. Season with salt, chile pepper, and the oil. Transfer to a serving dish.

Cook the pasta in a large pan of salted, boiling water until al dente, about 2–3 minutes.

Drain and place in the serving dish with the sauce, adding 2–3 tablespoons of the cooking water if the sauce is too dry. Toss gently and serve hot.

4 oz (125 g) peeled almonds, finely chopped
1 clove garlic, finely chopped
Salt
1 large bunch fresh basil
1 large ripe tomato, peeled, seeds removed, and chopped
1 dried chile pepper, crumbled, or $\frac{1}{2}$ teaspoon red pepper flakes
3 tablespoons extra-virgin olive oil
14 oz (400 g) fresh tagliolini

Spicy Tagliatelle
with creamy eggplant sauce

Boil the eggplants in lightly salted water for 4 minutes. Drain, squeezing out excess moisture.

Heat the oil in a large frying pan over medium heat. Add the garlic and thyme and sauté for 2 minutes. Add the eggplant and simmer for 6–7 minutes, mashing gently with a fork. Remove from the heat, add half the basil, and season with salt, pepper, and paprika. Chop in a food processor until smooth.

Return the eggplant cream to the pan and add the tomato. Cook until the tomatoes have broken down and the sauce is creamy.

Cook the pasta in a large pan of salted boiling water until al dente. Drain and add to the sauce. Add 2–3 tablespoons of cooking water, sprinkle with the cheese and remaining basil, and toss gently. Serve hot.

3 medium eggplants (aubergines,) peeled and chopped into small cubes

$1/3$ cup (90 ml) extra-virgin olive oil

2 cloves garlic, finely chopped

1 tablespoon finely chopped thyme

15 leaves fresh basil, torn

Salt and freshly ground white pepper

$1/2$ teaspoon hot paprika

3 ripe tomatoes, peeled and chopped

14 oz (400 g) fresh tagliatelle

6 tablespoons freshly grated pecorino romano cheese

SERVES 6–8

PREPARATION 45 min + 20 min to rest pasta

COOKING 35 min

DIFFICULTY level 3

Potato Ravioli
with pesto

Pasta: Place the flour on a work surface and make a well in the center. Pour the egg mixture into the well and mix to make a stiff dough. Knead for 15–20 minutes, until smooth and elastic. Cover and let rest for 20 minutes.

Pesto: Place the basil, pine nuts, garlic, oil, salt, and pepper in a food processor or blender and chop until smooth. Transfer the mixture to a medium bowl and stir in the cheese and water.

Filling: Boil the potatoes in a large pot of salted, boiling water until tender, 20 minutes. Drain and mash in a large bowl.

Mix the flour, milk, Parmesan, eggs, and marjoram into the potatoes.

Roll the pasta dough out on a lightly floured surface until very thin. Cut into 1 1/2 x 3-inch (4 x 8-cm) rectangles.

Put a teaspoonful of the filling on each rectangle, fold each one in half, and seal by pinching the edges together.

Cook the pasta in small batches in a large pot of salted, boiling water until al dente. Use a slotted spoon to drain the pasta and toss gently with the pesto.

Serve immediately.

Pasta

2 1/3 cups (350 g) all-purpose (plain) flour
1 large egg and 1 large egg yolk, lightly beaten with 1/3 cup (90 ml) water

Pesto

2 cups (45 g) fresh basil leaves
2 tablespoons pine nuts
2 cloves garlic
1/2 cup (125 ml) extra-virgin olive oil
Salt and freshly ground black pepper
4 tablespoons freshly grated Parmesan cheese
2 tablespoons boiling water

Filling

2 lb (1 kg) potatoes, peeled
1 cup (150 g) all-purpose (plain) flour
1/2 cup (125 ml) milk
1/2 cup (75 g) freshly grated Parmesan cheese
3 large eggs
2 teaspoons finely chopped fresh marjoram

Cannelloni
with tomatoes and cheese

Preheat the oven to 350°F (180°C/gas 4). Butter a baking dish.

Mix the ricotta, half the pecorino, half the basil, and the egg and egg yolk in a large bowl. Season with salt and pepper and mix well.

Cut the tomatoes in half horizontally. Arrange half of them in the prepared baking dish. Drizzle with 2 tablespoons of oil and season with salt, pepper, and the remaining basil. Sprinkle with 2 tablespoons of pecorino.

Spoon the ricotta mixture into the cannelloni. Arrange the cannelloni on top of the tomatoes, one next to the other. Season with salt and pepper and drizzle with 2 tablespoons oil. Sprinkle with 2 tablespoons of pecorino. Place the mozzarella on top of the cannelloni. Cover with the remaining halved tomatoes, cut-side down. Drizzle with the remaining oil and season with salt and pepper.

Cover with aluminum foil and bake for 20 minutes. Remove the foil and sprinkle with the remaining pecorino. Bake until golden brown, about 20 minutes. Serve hot.

2 cups (500 ml) fresh ricotta cheese, drained

1¼ cups (150 g) freshly grated pecorino cheese

1 tablespoon finely chopped basil

1 egg + 1 egg yolk

Salt and freshly ground black pepper

2 lb (1 kg) small or medium tomatoes

½ cup (125 ml) extra-virgin olive oil

10 oz (300 g) cannelloni pasta

5 oz (150 g) mozzarella cheese, diced

SERVES 4–6

PREPARATION 10 min

COOKING 35 min

DIFFICULTY level 1

Baked Pappardelle
with squash

Preheat the oven to 400°F (200°C/gas 6). Oil a large baking dish.

Sauté the garlic in the oil in a large frying pan over medium heat until pale gold. Add the squash and wine and simmer for 10 minutes. The squash should be tender.

Cook the pasta in a large pot of salted boiling water until al dente, 3–5 minutes. Drain and add to the squash. Simmer over medium heat for 2 minutes. Add the parsley and season with pepper. Discard the garlic.

Transfer the mixture to the prepared baking dish. Top with the Fontina and butter. Sprinkle with the Parmesan.

Bake until lightly browned, 10–15 minutes. Serve hot.

1 clove garlic, lightly crushed but whole
1/4 cup (60 ml) extra-virgin olive oil
12 oz (350 g) squash flesh, thinly sliced
1/2 cup (125 ml) dry white wine
14 oz (400 g) fresh pappardelle
1 tablespoon finely chopped parsley
Freshly ground black pepper
12 oz (350 g) freshly grated Fontina cheese
1 tablespoon butter
1/2 cup (75 g) freshly grated Parmesan cheese

SERVES 4

PREPARATION 30 min

COOKING 1 h 20 min

DIFFICULTY level 2

Mushroom Lasagne

Preheat the oven to 400°F (200°C/gas 6).

Cook the pasta in a large pan of salted, boiling water until al dente. Drain the pasta and lay the sheets out on a clean cloth, making sure that they do not overlap.

Sauté the carrots, celery, and shallots in the oil in a large frying pan over medium heat for 5–6 minutes. Add the tomatoes and simmer for 20 minutes.

Stir in the mushrooms and cook for 20 minutes more. Remove from the heat. Season with the salt and pepper.

Spoon a layer of mushroom mixture into an ovenproof dish. Cover with a layer of pasta. Cover with a layer of Fontina and sprinkle with Parmesan. Repeat until the dish is full. Finish with a cheese layer.

Bake until bubbling and golden brown, 30–35 minutes. Serve hot.

12 oz (350 g) fresh lasagne sheets
1 carrot, finely chopped
2 stalks celery, finely chopped
2 shallots, finely chopped
$\frac{1}{4}$ cup (60 ml) extra-virgin olive oil
14 oz (400 g) chopped tomatoes
1 lb (500 g) porcini (or other wild or white) mushrooms, coarsely chopped
Salt and freshly ground black pepper
8 oz (250 g) sliced Fontina cheese
1 cup (150 g) freshly grated Parmesan cheese

Potato Gnocchi

Boil the potatoes until tender, about 25 minutes, then slip off their skins. Mash or put through a potato ricer and place in a large bowl.

Beat the egg whites in a large bowl until stiff. Gently fold in the yolks, flour, salt, pepper, nutmeg, and, finally, the potatoes. Mix gently but thoroughly.

Bring a large saucepan of salted water to the boil and drop rounded spoonfuls of the potato mixture into the boiling water. Cook in small batches. When the gnocchi bob up to the surface, they are done. Scoop out with a slotted spoon and transfer to a heated serving dish. Sprinkle with the Parmesan.

Melt the butter and sage together in a small saucepan over low heat until the butter is pale golden brown.

Drizzle the flavored butter over the dumplings and serve hot.

1½ lb (750 g) floury potatoes, with peel
3 eggs, separated
1 cup (150 g) all-purpose (plain) flour
Salt and freshly ground white pepper
Freshly grated nutmeg
4 tablespoons freshly grated Parmesan cheese
½ cup (120 g) butter
10 fresh sage leaves

SERVES 4

PREPARATION 25 min + 30 min to rest

COOKING 15 min

DIFFICULTY level 2

Austrian Gnocchi

Heat the oil in a large frying pan over medium heat. Add the mushrooms and sauté until tender, 5–7 minutes. Set aside to cool.

Beat the butter and eggs in a medium bowl until pale in color. Add the cornstarch, parsley, and mushrooms and season with salt and pepper. Stir in enough bread crumbs to form a firm dough. Set aside to rest for 30 minutes.

Shape the dough into walnut-sized gnocchi (balls).

Cook the gnocchi in batches in a large saucepan of salted, boiling water until the bob up to the surface, 2–3 minutes each batch.

Scoop out with a slotted spoon and serve hot with the tomato sauce.

2 tablespoons extra-virgin olive oil
5 oz (150 g) mushrooms, finely chopped
⅓ cup (90 g) butter, melted
3 eggs
2 tablespoons corn starch (cornflour)
1 tablespoon finely chopped parsley
Salt and freshly ground black pepper
7 oz (200 g) bread crumbs
1 lb (500 g) tomato sauce, storebought or homemade (see page 100)

SERVES 4–6

PREPARATION 45 min + 1 h to rest

COOKING 20 min

DIFFICULTY level 2

Potato Gnocchi
with bell pepper sauce

Gnocchi: Cook the potatoes in a large pot of salted boiling water until tender, 20–25 minutes. Drain and let cool slightly.

Slip off their skins and mash until smooth. Gradually stir in the egg yolks and enough of the flour to obtain a soft but smooth dough that is just a little sticky.

Take a piece of dough and roll it on a lightly floured work surface into a "sausage" about 1/2 inch (1 cm) in diameter. Cut into pieces about 1 inch (2.5 cm) long. Repeat with all the dough. To give the gnocchi their special grooves, twist them around the tines of a fork.

Place the gnocchi on a lightly floured clean cloth well spaced so they do not stick together. Let rest for 1 hour.

Bell Pepper Sauce: Sauté the shallots in the oil in a large frying pan over medium heat until softened, 3–4 minutes. Add the capers, bell peppers, and tomatoes. Cover and simmer until the bell peppers are tender, about 10 minutes. Add the wine and let it evaporate for 1 minute. Season with salt and simmer for 30 minutes.

Set a large pot of salted water to boil. The gnocchi should be cooked in batches. Lower the first batch (20–24 gnocchi) gently into the boiling water. After a few minutes they will rise to the surface. Simmer for 1 minute, then scoop out with a slotted spoon. Place in a heated serving dish. Repeat until all the gnocchi are cooked.

Spoon the sauce over the gnocchi. Sprinkle with the butter and chives and serve hot.

Potato Gnocchi
2 lb (1 kg) starchy potatoes, with peel
2 large egg yolks
2 cups (300 g) all-purpose (plain) flour

Bell Pepper Sauce
2 shallots, thinly sliced
1/4 cup (60 ml) extra-virgin olive oil
2 tablespoons salt-cured capers, rinsed
2 large red bell peppers (capsicums), seeded and finely chopped
2 (14-oz/400-g) cans tomatoes, with juice
1/4 cup (60 ml) dry white wine
Salt
1 tablespoon butter, cut up
1 tablespoon snipped chives

Potato Gnocchi
and leek gratin

Prepare the gnocchi.

Preheat the oven to 400°F (200°C/gas 6). Grease one large or 4–6 individual ovenproof dishes.

Beat the cornstarch with a little of the cream in a small bowl. Stir in the rest of the cream. Melt the butter in a large frying pan over medium heat. Add the leeks and sauté until they begin to soften, 3–4 minutes.

Add 3 tablespoons of water and cook until the leeks are tender, about 5 minutes. Add the cognac and cook over high heat until it evaporates, 2–3 minutes. Lower the heat and stir in the cream and cornstarch. Simmer, stirring often, until thickened, about 5 minutes. Add the nutmeg and season with salt and pepper.

Cook the gnocchi in a large pan of salted, boiling water until they rise to the surface. Scoop out with a slotted spoon, draining well, and place in the prepared baking dish(es). Spoon the leek sauce over the top. Sprinkle with Parmesan.

Bake until lightly browned, 5–10 minutes. Garnish with the basil and serve hot.

1 quantity potato gnocchi (see page 128)
2 tablespoons butter
5 small leeks, thinly sliced
2 tablespoons cognac
1 tablespoon cornstarch (cornflour)
1¼ cups (300 ml) heavy (double) cream
¼ teaspoon freshly grated nutmeg
Salt and freshly ground black pepper
¾ cup (90 g) freshly grated Parmesan cheese
Sprigs of basil, to garnish

GRILLED VEGETABLES

SERVES 6

PREPARATION 15 min

COOKING 30 min

DIFFICULTY level 1

Vegetable Grill

Heat a grill pan over high heat.

Place the zucchini in the pan and grill until tender, about 5 minutes each side. Place the bell pepper strips in the grill pan and grill until tender, about 10 minutes. Place the eggplant slices in the grill pan and grill until tender, about 5 minutes each side.

Place all the grilled vegetables on a large serving plate. Season with salt and pepper. Drizzle with the oil and serve hot or at room temperature.

4 medium zucchini (courgettes), sliced lengthwise

1 red bell pepper (capsicum), seeded and cut in strips

1 yellow bell pepper (capsicum), seeded and cut in strips

1 large eggplant (aubergine), with peel, sliced

Salt and freshly ground black pepper

$1/3$ cup (90 ml) extra-virgin olive oil

Grilled Zucchini

Mix the oil, garlic, basil, chile powder, and salt in a small bowl.

Wash the zucchini, pat dry on paper towels, and slice finely lengthwise. Place in a shallow dish with the marinade and let marinate for about 1 hour.

Drain the marinade from the zucchini slices. Arrange the zucchini in small batches on a grill pan. Grill until tender, about 8 minutes, brushing with the marinade during cooking.

Transfer to a serving plate and serve hot.

⅓ cup (90 ml) extra-virgin olive oil
3 cloves garlic, finely chopped
1 small bunch fresh basil, torn
Chile powder, to taste
Salt
6 zucchini (courgettes)

Grilled Eggplant

Trim, rinse, and dry the eggplants. Slice thinly lengthwise and arrange in layers in a colander, sprinkling each layer with salt. Set aside for I hour.

Rinse the eggplants carefully and dry with paper towels.

Cook the eggplant in batches in a grill pan until tender, about I0 minutes.

Arrange in layers in a deep dish, placing slices of garlic and sage leaves between the layers of eggplant. Pour in enough wine vinegar to cover the top layer. Let marinate in the refrigerator for 24 hours.

4 medium-large eggplants (aubergines)
Coarse sea salt
$^1/_2$ cup (125 ml) olive oil, for frying
2 cloves garlic, thinly sliced
8–10 leaves fresh sage
High-quality wine vinegar, to serve

Grilled Onions
with bay leaves

Blanch the onions in a pot of salted, boiling water for 5 minutes. Drain, dry, and thread onto 4 skewers (5 onions each, alternated with a half bay leaf). Skewer the onions horizontally so that they will lie flat in the grill pan during cooking.

Drizzle with oil and cook in a hot grill pan, turning often. Cook until the onions are tender and golden brown, about 15 minutes.

Season with salt and pepper and serve hot.

20 small white onions, peeled
8 bay leaves, cut in half
3 tablespoons extra-virgin olive oil
Salt and freshly ground black pepper

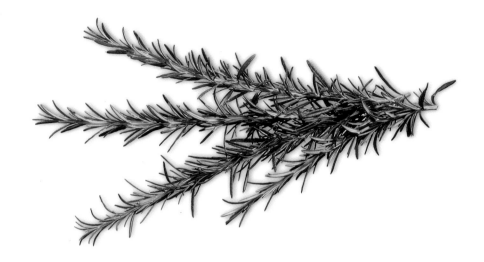

Vegetable Skewers

Cut the zucchini in thick wheels. Chop the eggplant in thick slices, then divide in 4. Divide the onion in 4 wedges, then cut each wedge in half. Cut the bell peppers in 1-inch (2.5-cm) squares.

Thread the vegetable pieces onto wooden skewers. Set them on a plate. Prepare at least two skewers per person.

Place the oil, salt, pepper, paprika, lemon juice, and herbs in a small bowl and beat vigorously with a fork until well mixed. Pour over the skewers, cover with aluminum foil, and marinate in the refrigerator for 2 hours.

Heat a grill pan over high heat until very hot, drain the skewers, and place half of them in the pan. Grill, turning so that they brown on all sides, until tender, about 10 minutes.

Serve hot.

2 zucchini (courgettes)
1 eggplant (aubergine)
1 medium onion
1 small red, 1 small yellow, and 1 small green bell pepper (capsicum)
5 tablespoons extra-virgin olive oil
Salt and freshly ground black pepper
$\frac{1}{2}$ teaspoon hot paprika
Freshly squeezed juice of $\frac{1}{2}$ lemon
1 teaspoon dried or 1 tablespoon finely chopped fresh herbs (oregano, mint, or thyme)

Vegetable Kebabs
with mozzarella

Arrange the zucchini and eggplant in a grill pan and grill until tender, 7–10 minutes.

Thread the vegetables onto wooden skewers alternating with the mozzarella, tomatoes, and basil leaves. Season with salt and pepper and brush with the oil.

Cook on the grill until the cheese and tomatoes are heated through, about 5 minutes.

Serve hot.

2 zucchini (courgettes), thickly sliced
1 medium eggplant (aubergine), thickly sliced
8 baby mozzarella cheeses (bocconcini)
16 cherry tomatoes
8 leaves fresh basil
Salt and freshly ground black pepper
$1/4$ cup (60 ml) extra-virgin olive oil

Zucchini
with arugula pesto

Rinse the zucchini thoroughly under cold running water and dry well. Trim the ends off the zucchini and cut lengthwise in very thin slices. Place in a small, shallow dish.

Mix 2 tablespoons of oil, cider vinegar, balsamic vinegar, garlic, salt, and pepper in a small bowl. Pour the mixture over the zucchini. Let marinate for 1 hour.

Place 3 oz (90 g) of the arugula in a blender with 4 tablespoons of pine nuts and the remaining oil and chop until smooth. If the mixture is not liquid enough, add 1–2 tablespoons hot water.

Drain the zucchini, setting aside the marinade. Heat a large grill pan over medium heat. Cook the zucchini in batches until tender, 4–5 minutes each batch.

Arrange the remaining arugula on a serving platter and place the zucchini on top. Sprinkle with the remaining 2 tablespoons of pine nuts and the raisins. Season with salt and pepper and drizzle with the marinade.

Serve hot or at room temperature.

$1\frac{1}{2}$ lb (750 g) small zucchini (courgettes)
$\frac{1}{4}$ cup (60 ml) extra-virgin olive oil
2 tablespoons cider vinegar
1 tablespoon balsamic vinegar
1 clove garlic, thinly sliced
Salt and freshly ground black pepper
4 oz (125 g) arugula (rocket)
6 tablespoons pine nuts
4 tablespoons raisins

Grilled Tomatoes
with garlic and herb cheese sauce

Mix the goat cheese, thyme, marjoram, chives, and spring onion in a medium bowl until smooth. Stir in the vinegar and wine. Place in the refrigerator.

Preheat a broiler (grill) to a high setting. Arrange the tomatoes on a large baking sheet. Stick a piece of garlic and rosemary into each tomato half and drizzle with the oil. Season with salt and pepper.

Grill until the tomatoes have softened slightly, 5–10 minutes.

Serve hot with the herb cheese sauce.

1$\frac{1}{4}$ cups (300 g) creamy fresh goat cheese
1 tablespoon finely chopped thyme
1 tablespoon finely chopped marjoram
1 tablespoon snipped chives
1 spring onion, white part only, thinly sliced
3 tablespoons white wine vinegar
3 tablespoons dry white wine
12 small, ripe tomatoes, cut in half
2 cloves garlic, sliced
24 tiny sprigs rosemary
$\frac{1}{4}$ cup (60 ml) extra-virgin olive oil
Salt and freshly ground black pepper

VEGETABLE STEWS & STIR-FRIES

Mushrooms
with pine nuts

Sauté the potatoes and garlic in the oil in a large frying pan over medium heat for 5 minutes.

Add the mushrooms and season with salt and pepper. Cover and simmer for 5 minutes. Uncover and let some of the moisture evaporate. Stir in the pine nuts and almonds and simmer for 10–15 more minutes.

Sprinkle with the mint just before removing from the heat. Serve hot.

2 large potatoes, peeled and diced
2 cloves garlic, finely chopped
1/4 cup (60 ml) extra-virgin olive oil
1 1/2 lb (750 g) white mushrooms, coarsely chopped
Salt and freshly ground black pepper
2/3 cup (150 g) pine nuts
1/2 cup (100 g) slivered almonds
1 tablespoon coarsely chopped mint

Mushroom Curry

Chop the cashew nuts with ½ cup (125 ml) of water in a food processor until smooth.

Warm the oil in a large frying pan over medium heat. Sauté the cinnamon and cardamon until fragrant. Add the onion, ginger, and garlic and sauté for 3 minutes. Add the tomatoes, cilantro, chile, turmeric, and garam masala and simmer over low heat until the oil begins to separate, about 10 minutes.

Add the salt and water. Bring to a boil. Stir in the mushrooms, peas, and cashew nut mixture. Simmer, stirring occasionally, until the vegetables are tender, about 10 minutes. Serve hot.

- 3 oz (90 g) cashew nuts
- 2 cups (500 ml) water
- 2 tablespoons peanut oil
- 1 cinnamon stick, halved
- 5 cardamons
- 1 onion, sliced
- 1 tablespoon chopped root ginger
- 2 cloves garlic, finely chopped
- 4 tomatoes, chopped
- 2 teaspoons ground coriander
- 1 green chile pepper, seeded and finely sliced
- 1 teaspoon ground turmeric
- 2 teaspoons garam masala
- 1 teaspoon salt
- 14 oz (400 g) white mushrooms, coarsely chopped
- 1 cup (150 g) frozen peas

SERVES 4–6

PREPARATION 10 min

COOKING 20 min

DIFFICULTY level 1

Mushrooms
with potatoes with herbs

Sauté 1 tablespoon each of the parsley and marjoram in 3 tablespoons of oil in a large frying pan over medium heat for 1 minute. Add the potatoes and 1 clove of garlic. Sauté until the potatoes are almost tender, 5–10 minutes.

Heat the remaining oil in a large frying pan over medium heat. Add 1 tablespoon of parsley and the remaining marjoram and sauté for 1 minute. Add the wild mushrooms and the remaining garlic and sauté for 2 minutes.

Add the button mushrooms to the pan with the potatoes. Sauté until the mushrooms and potatoes are tender, 5–7 minutes.

Combine the two mixtures and season with salt and pepper. Sprinkle with the remaining parsley. Serve hot.

3 tablespoons finely chopped parsley
2 tablespoons finely chopped marjoram
1/3 cup (90 ml) extra-virgin olive oil
2 cloves garlic, finely chopped
1 lb (500 g) potatoes, peeled and cut into small chunks
1 lb (500 g) wild mushrooms, thinly sliced
12 oz (350 g) button mushrooms, thinly sliced
Salt and freshly ground black pepper

Peppers
Fennel

Sautéed Vegetables
with egg white omelet

Beat the egg whites and ¼ teaspoon salt in a large bowl until stiff.

Melt 1 tablespoon of butter in a wok or frying pan over medium heat. Pour in the beaten whites and cook until set. Turn out onto a board and cut into thin strips.

Sauté the spring onion in the remaining butter in a wok or frying pan over medium heat until lightly browned. Add the carrots and stir-fry for 2–3 minutes. Season with salt. Pour in the water and simmer until tender, 8–10 minutes.

Stir-fry the thyme and marjoram in the oil in a wok or frying pan for 1–2 minutes. Add the asparagus and fava beans and stir-fry until tender, 5–7 minutes.

Stir in the carrots and parsley. Stir-fry for 1 minute.

Add the omelet strips and sprinkle with the Parmesan. Serve hot.

8 egg whites
Salt
1 spring onion, finely chopped
3 tablespoons butter
8 oz (250 g) carrots, peeled and cut into thin sticks
1 cup (250 ml) water
1 tablespoon finely chopped thyme
1 tablespoon finely chopped marjoram
2 tablespoons extra-virgin olive oil
1 lb (500 g) asparagus tips, cut in half
4 oz (125 g) fresh fava (broad) beans
1 tablespoon finely chopped parsley
1 tablespoon freshly grated Parmesan cheese

Sicilian Eggplant

Soak the eggplant in a large bowl of cold water with the lemon juice for 15 minutes. Drain and pat dry with a kitchen towel.

Sauté the eggplant in half the oil in a large frying pan over medium heat until lightly browned.

Sauté the onions and celery in the remaining oil in a large frying pan until golden. Add the tomatoes, eggplant, and capers. Cover and simmer for 15 minutes. Add the sugar and vinegar and simmer until the vinegar has evaporated.

Garnish with the mint and let cool to room temperature before serving.

2 eggplant (aubergines), cut into small cubes
Freshly squeezed juice of 2 lemons
1/3 cup (90 ml) extra-virgin olive oil
2 medium onions, thinly sliced
1 stalk celery, finely chopped
4 tomatoes, seeded and coarsely chopped
3 tablespoons salt-cured capers, rinsed
2 tablespoons sugar
1/4 cup (60 ml) vinegar
2 sprigs mint, to garnish

Pineapple Curry
with coconut

Spice Paste: Grind the chilies, coriander seeds, garlic, shallots, turmeric, and ginger root in a pestle and mortar until crushed.

Curry: Heat the oil in a large wok or frying pan and sauté the spice paste until aromatic, 1–2 minutes. Pour in the coconut milk and bring to a boil, stirring constantly.

Add the pineapple, star anise, cinnamon, cloves, nutmeg, lemongrass, and lime juice. Season with salt and pepper. Cook over medium heat until the pineapple is heated through, 5–7 minutes. Stir in the coconut cream and cook for 2–3 minutes more.

Garnish with the fried shallots and serve hot.

Spice Paste
4–6 dried red chile peppers, crumbled
1 teaspoon coriander seeds
2 cloves garlic, finely chopped
6 shallots, finely chopped
1 teaspoon ground turmeric
1 tablespoon finely chopped fresh ginger

Curry
2 tablespoons extra-virgin olive oil
3 cups (750 ml) coconut milk
1 ripe pineapple, peeled and cut
    into small cubes
2 star anise, chopped
One 3-inch (8-cm) stick cinnamon
$1/4$ teaspoon ground cloves
$1/8$ teaspoon ground nutmeg
1 stalk lemongrass, finely chopped
1 tablespoon freshly squeezed lime juice
Salt and freshly ground black pepper
$1/2$ cup (125 ml) coconut cream
2 shallots, finely chopped and lightly fried,
    to garnish

SERVES 4–6

PREPARATION 20min

COOKING 35-45 min

DIFFICULTY level 1

Vegetarian Tajine

Blanch the tomatoes in a large pot of salted, boiling water for 1 minute. Peel, gently squeeze out as many seeds as possible, then chop the flesh into small cubes.

Sauté the onions and whole spring onion bulbs in half the oil over medium heat in a tajine or heavy-bottomed pan until lightly browned. Add the tomatoes, carrots, and zucchini. Sauté for 10 minutes.

Add the remaining oil, cumin seeds, cinnamon, cloves, half the mint, and the herbs. Pour in the vegetable stock and season with salt and pepper. Simmer until the vegetables are tender, about 20 minutes.

Garnish with the remaining mint and serve hot.

3 tomatoes
2 onions, coarsely chopped
4 spring onions, bulbs only
$\frac{1}{3}$ cup (90 ml) extra-virgin olive oil
3 carrots, cut into rounds
3 zucchini (courgettes), cut into small pieces
1 teaspoon cumin seeds
$\frac{1}{4}$ teaspoon ground cinnamon
$\frac{1}{8}$ teaspoon ground cloves
1 tablespoon finely chopped mint
1 bunch mixed fresh herbs, finely chopped
2 cups (500 ml) vegetable stock
Salt and freshly ground black pepper

Tofu
with mushrooms

Heat the frying oil in a wok to very hot. Fry the bean curd in two batches until golden brown all over, 5–7 minutes. Drain on paper towels. Discard the frying oil.

Stir-fry the spring onions and ginger in the 3 tablespoons of peanut oil in the wok over medium heat for 5 minutes. Add the mushrooms and stir-fry for 5 more minutes.

Stir in the bamboo shoots, vegetable stock, soy sauce, sesame oil, and the fried bean curd. Season with the pepper. Simmer for 3 minutes. Add the bok choy and simmer for 2–3 minutes.

Mix the cornstarch and water in a small bowl. Stir into the tofu mixture to thicken. Transfer to a heated serving dish and serve hot.

1 cup (250 ml) olive oil, for frying

2 lb (1 kg) tofu (bean curd), cut into small chunks

3 tablespoons peanut oil

2 spring onions, thinly sliced

1 tablespoon finely chopped fresh ginger root

1 lb (500 g) button mushrooms

$\frac{1}{2}$ cup (125 g) finely sliced bamboo shoots

1 cup (250 ml) vegetable stock

$2\frac{1}{2}$ tablespoons soy sauce

1 teaspoon sesame oil

Freshly ground black pepper

4 bok choy, cooked and cut in half

2 teaspoons cornstarch (cornflour)

1 tablespoon water

Bell Pepper Stew

Heat the oil in a large frying pan over medium heat. Add the onion and sauté until softened, 3–4 minutes.

Add the tomatoes and bell peppers and mix well. Simmer until the peppers are very tender and the sauce has reduced, about 30 minutes.

Stir in the vinegar. Simmer until the vinegar has evaporated, 5 minutes. Add the olives and season with salt. Mix well and simmer for 5 minutes.

Serve warm or at room temperature.

$1/3$ cup (90 ml) extra-virgin olive oil

6 onions, thinly sliced

2 (14-oz/400-g) cans tomatoes, with juice

2 red bell peppers (capsicums), seeded and sliced

2 yellow peppers (capsicums), seeded and sliced

2 green bell peppers (capsicums), seeded and sliced

$1/3$ cup (90 ml) white wine vinegar

1 cup (100 g) pitted green olives, coarsely chopped

Salt

Spicy Tofu

Soak the dried mushrooms in warm water for 15 minutes. Soak the tofu strips in warm water for 15 minutes. Chop the soaked tofu finely and set aside.

Heat the oil in a large wok or frying pan over medium heat. Stir-fry the celery and garlic for 5 minutes. Add the mushrooms and chilies and stir-fry for 3 minutes.

Stir in the tofu vegetable stock, soy sauce, sesame oil, and sugar. Simmer until the liquid has reduced slightly, about 5 minutes.

Mix the water and cornstarch in a small bowl. Stir into the wok to thicken the mixture. Season with pepper, garnish with the parsley, and serve hot.

2 teaspoons dried black mushrooms
2 teaspoons dried tofu (bean curd) strips
2 tablespoons peanut oil
2 stalks celery, finely chopped
2 cloves garlic, peeled and finely chopped
2 red chile peppers, finely chopped
2 lb (1 kg) tofu (bean curd), cut into
   $\frac{1}{2}$-inch (1-cm) cubes
$1\frac{1}{2}$ cups (375 ml) vegetable stock
1 tablespoon soy sauce
1 tablespoon sesame oil
$\frac{1}{2}$ teaspoon sugar
1 tablespoon water
1 teaspoon cornstarch (cornflour)
Freshly ground black pepper
1 tablespoon finely chopped parsley

Sweet Tofu

Heat the oil a large wok or frying pan over medium-high heat. Stir-fry the tofu half the spring onions, half the garlic, and ginger for 5 minutes. Add the chilies and stir-fry for 1 minute.

Stir in the sherry, soy sauce, 1 cup (250 ml) of water, and salt. Bring to a boil and simmer for 3 minutes.

Mix the remaining water and cornstarch in a small bowl. Stir into the tofu mixture to thicken. Sprinkle with the remaining spring onion and garlic.

Transfer to a heated serving dish and serve hot.

2 tablespoons peanut oil
2 lb (1 kg) tofu (bean curd, cut into
   $\frac{1}{2}$-inch (1-cm) cubes
2 spring onions, finely chopped
2 cloves garlic, finely chopped
1 teaspoon finely chopped fresh ginger root
2 small red chile peppers, finely chopped
1 tablespoon dry sherry
$1\frac{1}{2}$ tablespoons soy sauce
1 cup (250 ml) + 1 tablespoon water
$\frac{1}{2}$ teaspoon salt
$1\frac{1}{2}$ teaspoons cornstarch (cornflour)

Couscous
with bell peppers and potatoes

Heat the oil in a large saucepan over medium heat. Add the onion, cumin, and garlic and sauté until the onions are softened, about 5 minutes.

Add the paprika, tomatoes, sugar, salt, chile powder, coriander, garam masala, vegetable stock, bell peppers, eggplant, and zucchini. Stir everything together over medium heat for a few minutes. Cover and simmer until all the vegetables are tender, about 25 minutes.

Stir in the parsley, dill, olives, and apricots and cook until heated through.

Pile the couscous high on a large serving platter. Spoon the vegetables over the top and serve hot.

1/4 cup (60 ml) extra-virgin olive oil
1 large white onion, finely chopped
1/2 teaspoon cumin seeds
2 cloves garlic, finely chopped
1 teaspoon sweet paprika
1 (14-oz/400-g) can tomatoes, with juice
1 teaspoon sugar
1 teaspoon salt
1 teaspoon chile powder
2 tablespoons ground coriander
1 teaspoon garam masala
2 cups (500 ml) vegetable stock
3 bell peppers (capsicums), mixed colors, seeded and thinly sliced
2 baby eggplants (aubergines), with peel, chopped
2 zucchini (courgettes), sliced lengthwise
2 medium potatoes, cut in small dice
2 tablespoons finely chopped parsley
1 tablespoon finely chopped dill
10 black olives
5 dried apricots, coarsely chopped
Freshly cooked couscous, to serve

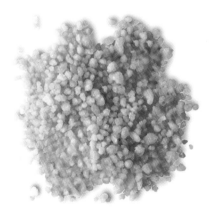

Vegetarian Chile
with yogurt and cilantro

Heat the oil in a large saucepan over medium heat. Add the cumin seeds and toast until fragrant, about 2 minutes. Add the onions, celery, garlic, and green curry paste and cook until the onions are softened, about 5 minutes.

Add the bell peppers, zucchini, eggplant, mushrooms, and tomatoes. Cover and simmer over medium heat until the vegetables begin to soften, about 5 minutes.

Add the tomato purée, chile sauce, chile powder, cumin, coriander, and salt. Mix well, then add the kidney beans. Cover and cook until the vegetables are tender, about 25 minutes. Stir occasionally during cooking.

Stir in the yogurt, lemon juice, and cilantro. Serve hot over the rice.

2 tablespoons extra-virgin olive oil

I teaspoon cumin seeds

I large onion, finely sliced

2 stalks celery, chopped

2 cloves garlic, finely chopped

I teaspoon green curry paste

$\frac{1}{2}$ red bell pepper (capsicum), seeded and sliced

$\frac{1}{2}$ green bell pepper (capsicum), seeded and sliced

2 zucchini (courgettes), sliced

I medium eggplant (aubergine), chopped, with peel

8 oz (250 g) mushrooms, quartered

2 (14-oz/400-g) cans tomatoes, chopped, with juice

I tablespoon tomato purée

I tablespoon sweet chile sauce

I teaspoon chile powder

I teaspoon ground cumin seeds

2 teaspoons ground coriander

I teaspoon salt

I (14-oz/400 g) can red kidney beans, drained

I tablespoon plain yogurt

Juice of I lemon

Handful of finely chopped cilantro (coriander)

Freshly cooked basmati rice, to serve

Vegetarian Curry
with brown rice

Heat the oil over medium heat in a large saucepan. Add the mustard and cumin seeds and stir until fragrant, about 3 minutes. Add the chiles, garlic, ginger, and onions and sauté until softened, about 5 minutes.

Stir in the marrow or zucchini, potatoes, okra, winter squash, and mushrooms. Add the white pepper, salt, Worcestershire sauce, and soy sauce. Pour in the stock, cover, and simmer until the vegetables are tender, about 30 minutes. The liquid should reduce a little and the vegetables should be tender.

Stir in the cream and simmer for 5 minutes more. Garnish with the coriander and serve hot over the brown rice.

2 tablespoons peanut oil

$\frac{1}{2}$ teaspoon mustard seeds

$\frac{1}{2}$ teaspoon cumin seeds

2 green chiles, cut into slivers

2 cloves garlic, finely chopped

1 teaspoon minced fresh ginger

2 onions, finely chopped

1 marrow or 4 large zucchini (courgettes), cut into bite-size pieces

2 large potatoes, peeled and cut in bite-size chunks

4 oz (125 g) okra, sliced

4 oz (125 g) winter squash or pumpkin, peeled, seeded, and cubed

4 oz (125 g) button mushrooms, chopped

$\frac{1}{2}$ teaspoon white pepper

1 teaspoon salt

1 tablespoon Worcestershire sauce

2 tablespoons dark soy sauce

2 cups (500 ml) boiling vegetable stock or water

$\frac{1}{2}$ cup (125 ml) light (single) cream

Handful of finely chopped cilantro (coriander), to garnish

Freshly cooked brown rice, to serve

SERVES 4–6

PREPARATION 10 min

COOKING 30 min

DIFFICULTY level 1

Vegetable Curry
with couscous

Heat the oil in a tajine or saucepan over medium-high heat. Add the onions and garlic and sauté until softened, about 5 minutes.

Add the bell peppers, eggplant, potatoes, marrow, corn, and garbanzo beans. Stir well and sauté until the vegetables begin to soften, about 5 minutes.

Add the salt, pepper, chiles, tomatoes, harissa, cumin, and stock. Stir well and cover tightly, allowing no steam to escape. Reduce the heat and simmer over very low heat until the vegetables are tender, 30 minutes Sprinkle with the cilantro and serve hot with the couscous.

3 tablespoons extra-virgin olive oil

1 red onion, finely chopped

1 white onion, finely chopped

2 cloves garlic, finely chopped

3 bell peppers (capsicum), mixed colors, seeded and sliced

2 medium eggplant (aubergines), unpeeled and chopped

4 medium-large potatoes, unpeeled and chopped into bite-size pieces

1 small marrow or 2 large zucchini (courgettes), sliced

8 baby corns (sweet corns)

1 (14-oz/400-g) can garbanzo beans (chickpeas), drained

1 teaspoon salt

$1/2$ teaspoon freshly ground black pepper

1–2 fresh red chiles, finely chopped

1 (14-oz/400-g) can tomatoes, with juice

1 tablespoon tomato purée

1 tablespoon harissa

$1/2$ teaspoon cumin seeds

2 cups (500 ml) vegetable stock

2 tablespoons finely chopped cilantro (coriander)

Freshly cooked couscous, to serve

SERVES 6

PREPARATION 15 min + 1 h to drain

COOKING 12 min

DIFFICULTY level 1

Eggplant
with basil

Place the eggplant in a colander. Sprinkle with the coarse sea salt and let drain for 1 hour.

Stir-fry the garlic and chile pepper in the peanut oil in a wok or large frying pan over medium heat for 2 minutes. Add the eggplant and stir-fry until tender, 5–10 minutes.

Add the soy sauce, sugar, vinegar, salt, and basil and mix well. Drizzle with the sesame oil and serve hot.

- 1 lb (500 g) eggplant (aubergines), cut into bite-size chunks
- 1–2 tablespoons coarse sea salt
- 1 teaspoon finely chopped garlic
- 1 teaspoon finely chopped red chile pepper
- 3 tablespoons peanut oil
- 2 tablespoons soy sauce
- 1½ tablespoons sugar
- 1 tablespoon white wine vinegar
- ½ teaspoon salt
- 1 large bunch fresh basil, torn
- 1 tablespoon sesame oil

SERVES 4

PREPARATION 15 min

COOKING 35 min

DIFFICULTY level 1

Potato Curry

with coconut

Toast the cumin, fenugreek, and chile peppers in a medium saucepan for 2–3 minutes. Add the onion and 1 tablespoon of ghee. Stir-fry over high heat for 2–3 minutes.

Remove from the heat and process in a food processor or blender with 2 tablespoons of water until smooth.

Melt the remaining ghee in the same pan and stir-fry the curry leaves and mustard seeds for 30 seconds. Stir in the spice paste, potatoes, turmeric, coconut, and the remaining water. Season with salt.

Cover and simmer over low heat until the potatoes are tender, 25–30 minutes. Add more water during the cooking time if the sauce dries out.

Serve hot.

1 lb (500 g) new potatoes, sliced
1 teaspoon cumin seeds
$\frac{1}{2}$ teaspoon fenugreek seeds
2 dried red chile peppers, crumbled
1 onion, finely sliced
3 tablespoons ghee (clarified butter)
1 cup (250 ml) water + extra,
    as required
8 curry leaves
1 teaspoon mustard seeds
$\frac{1}{2}$ teaspoon ground turmeric
2 tablespoons shredded (desiccated) coconut
Salt

Sautéed Peas
with onion and fennel seeds

Cook the peas in salted boiling water until tender, 10–15 minutes. Drain well.

Sauté the onion in the oil in a large frying pan over low heat until light golden brown, 5–7 minutes. Add the peas and fennel seeds. Season with salt and pepper. Sauté over high heat for 3–4 minutes.

Sprinkle with the basil and parsley. Serve hot.

1 lb (500 g) hulled (shelled) peas
1 onion, finely chopped
$1/4$ cup (60 ml) extra-virgin olive oil
1 tablespoon fennel seeds, crushed
Salt and freshly ground white pepper
1 tablespoon torn basil
1 tablespoon finely chopped parsley

Chinese Vegetables
with omelet

Mix 1 tablespoon of water, 1 tablespoon of soy sauce, 1 teaspoon of cornstarch, and the white wine in a large bowl. Add the bean curd and let marinate for 10 minutes. Stir in 1 tablespoon of oil. Chop the soaked bean thread into short lengths.

Rinse the chive and spinach thoroughly under cold running water and dry well. Chop into short lengths.

Heat a large wok over medium heat and add 3 tablespoons of oil. Stir-fry the tofu for 3 minutes. Remove from the wok and set aside. Stir-fry the chive and spinach for 3 minutes, or until slightly wilted. Remove from the wok and set aside.

Add 1 tablespoon of oil and stir-fry the spring onions until lightly browned. Add the bean thread, vegetable stock, remaining soy sauce, and 1/2 teaspoon salt. Simmer until the sauce has reduced, then stir in the bean sprouts. Cook for 3 more minutes then add the bean curd mixture. Transfer to a serving dish.

Beat the eggs with the remaining water, cornstarch, and salt in a medium bowl until frothy.

Heat the remaining oil in a large frying pan over medium heat. Pour in the beaten egg mixture, tilting the pan so that the batter thinly covers the bottom. Cook until light golden brown on the underside. Use a large spatula to flip the omelet and cook until golden.

Drape the omelet over the top of the serving dish. Serve hot.

- 2 tablespoons water
- 2 tablespoons soy sauce
- 2 teaspoons cornstarch (cornflour)
- 1 teaspoon white wine
- 4 oz (125 g) tofu (bean curd), coarsely chopped
- 1/3 cup (90 ml) peanut oil
- 2 oz (60 g) dried bean thread, soaked in warm water for 10 minutes and drained
- 2 oz (60 g) yellow chives
- 4 oz (125 g) fresh spinach leaves, stalks removed
- 1 cup (250 ml) vegetable stock
- 3/4 teaspoon salt
- 6 spring onions, finely chopped
- 4 oz (125 g) bean sprouts
- 3 eggs, lightly beaten

Veggie Stir-Fry

Heat the oil in a wok or frying pan over high heat. Add the garlic and stir-fry until pale gold. Add the zucchini, spring onions, and fava beans and stir-fry until the vegetables are tender, about 5 minutes.

Add the raisins and basil and stir in the sherry. Stir-fry for 1–2 minutes more. Season with salt and pepper.

Serve hot.

1/4 cup (60 ml) extra-virgin olive oil
2 cloves garlic, finely chopped
3 zucchini (courgettes), finely chopped
8 spring onions, white part only, sliced
5 oz (150 g) fresh or frozen fava (broad) beans
2 tablespoons golden raisins (sultanas)
6–8 leaves basil, torn
1/4 cup (60 ml) dry sherry
Salt and freshly ground black pepper

GRATINS & CASSEROLES

SERVES 4

PREPARATION 20 min

COOKING 45 min

DIFFICULTY level 1

Clafoutis
with vegetables and cheese

Preheat the oven to 350°F (180°C/gas 4).

Sauté the shallot in the oil in a large frying pan over medium heat until softened. Add the zucchini, carrots, asparagus, and fava beans and cook for 5 minutes. Season with the salt.

Oil two baking sheets. Place the bread on the baking sheets and dust with the paprika. Toast in the oven until lightly browned. Remove and set aside.

Mix the flour and milk in a small bowl. Heat the cream and eggs in a medium saucepan over medium heat, stirring constantly. Add the milk mixture and stir until the sauce begins to thicken.

Line the base of a large baking dish with the toast and cover with the Brie. Spoon the vegetables over the top. Pour the sauce over the top and sprinkle with the Parmesan.

Bake until the vegetables are tender and the topping is nicely browned, about 20–25 minutes. Serve hot.

1 shallot, finely chopped
1/4 cup (60 ml) extra-virgin olive oil
3 oz (90 g) zucchini (courgettes), cut into small cubes
3 oz (90 g) carrots, cut into small cubes
3 oz (90 g) asparagus tips, chopped
3 oz (90 g) fresh fava (broad) beans
Salt
6–8 slices firm-textured bread
1 teaspoon sweet paprika
1 tablespoon all-purpose (plain) flour
1/3 cup (90 ml) milk
1/3 cup (90 ml) heavy (double) cream
2 eggs, lightly beaten
5 oz (150 g) Brie cheese, thinly sliced
1 cup (125 g) freshly grated Parmesan cheese

Potato Bake
with tomatoes and oregano

Preheat the oven to 400°F (200°C/gas 6). Oil a large ovenproof dish.

Heat 2 tablespoons of the oil in a large frying pan over medium heat. Add the onion and sauté until softened, 4–5 minutes. Add the potatoes and sauté for 5 minutes. Season with salt and pepper.

Transfer to the ovenproof dish. Arrange the tomatoes in a layer on top of the potatoes. Sprinkle with oregano and bread crumbs. Drizzle with the remaining oil.

Bake until the potatoes are tender, 35–40 minutes. Serve hot.

$1/3$ cup (90 ml) extra-virgin olive oil

1 large onion, finely chopped

$1\frac{1}{2}$ lb (750 g) potatoes, peeled and thinly sliced

Salt and freshly ground black pepper

12 oz (350 g) cherry tomatoes, halved

$1/2$ teaspoon dried oregano

$1/2$ cup (60 g) fine dry bread crumbs

SERVES 4–6

PREPARATION 15 min

COOKING 1 hour

DIFFICULTY level 1

Baked Potato
with cabbage and cumin

Cook the potatoes in a large pot of salted boiling water until tender, 20–25 minutes. Drain well. Mash two-thirds of the potatoes. Cut the remaining potatoes into bite-size pieces. Place the potatoes in a bowl.

Preheat the oven to 350°F (180°C/gas 4). Grease a 10-inch (25-cm) baking pan.

Heat the oil in a large frying pan over medium heat. Add the garlic and cabbage and sauté until the cabbage is tender, 10–15 minutes.

Add the cabbage to the potatoes and mix gently. Add the eggs, mozzarella, half the cumin, and Parmesan. Season with salt and pepper. Mix well.

Spoon the mixture into the prepared pan and level the surface with the back of a spoon. Sprinkle with the remaining cumin seeds.

Bake until lightly browned, 35–40 minutes. Serve hot.

2 lb (1 kg) starchy (baking) potatoes, peeled

3 tablespoons extra-virgin olive oil

2 cloves garlic, finely chopped

12 oz (350 g) savoy cabbage, coarsely chopped

3 eggs, lightly beaten

5 oz (150 g) mozzarella, cut into small cubes

1 teaspoon cumin seeds

1/2 cup (60 g) freshly grated Parmesan cheese

Salt and freshly ground black pepper

SERVES 4–6

PREPARATION 15 min

COOKING 50 min

DIFFICULTY level 1

Potato Cakes

with goat cheese

Preheat the oven to 350°F (180°C/gas 4). Grease a 12-cup muffin pan.

Place a few marjoram leaves in the base of each muffin cup. Add a layer of potato. Add a little cheese and then another layer of potato. Repeat until all the potatoes and cheese are used. Finish with a layer of potato. Dot with butter. Season with salt.

Cover the muffin pan with aluminum foil. Bake for 40 minutes. Remove the foil. Increase the oven temperature to 400°F (200°C/gas 6).

Bake until golden brown, 5–10 minutes. Serve hot.

8 small sprigs marjoram

6 medium starchy (baking) potatoes, peeled and thinly sliced

8 oz (250 g) soft creamy goat cheese

2 tablespoons butter

Salt

Potato Roulade
with spinach

Cook the potatoes in a large pot of salted boiling water until tender, 20–25 minutes. Drain and mash in a large bowl.

Cook the spinach in salted boiling until tender, 4–5 minutes. Drain well and chop finely.

Mix the spinach, ricotta, 1 egg yolk, half the Parmesan, and the nutmeg in a bowl. Season with salt and pepper.

Add the remaining egg yolk, remaining Parmesan, the flour, and a pinch of salt to the bowl with the potatoes and mix well.

Roll out the potato mixture on a sheet of parchment paper to 1/4 inch (5 mm) thick. Spread the spinach mixture over the potato, leaving a 1-inch (2.5-cm) border around the edges.

Carefully roll up the roulade using the parchment paper to help you. Wrap the roulade securely in the paper and seal the ends, tying with kitchen string.

Put the roulade into a large casserole and cover with boiling water. Simmer gently for 20 minutes.

Remove from the heat and drain. Let the roulade cool completely before unwrapping it.

Melt the butter with the sage in a small saucepan.

Unwrap and slice the roulade. Arrange on a serving dish. Drizzle with the butter and serve.

1 lb (500 g) starchy (baking) potatoes, peeled
12 oz (350 g) fresh spinach, well washed
5 oz (150 g) ricotta cheese, drained
2 large egg yolks, lightly beaten
1/2 cup (60 g) freshly grated Parmesan
1/4 teaspoon freshly grated nutmeg
Salt and freshly ground black pepper
2/3 cup (100 g) fine polenta (stoneground corn)
1/4 cup (60 g) butter
6 sage leaves

Zucchini Lasagne

Preheat the oven to 400°F (200°C/gas 6).

Heat 2 tablespoons of oil in a large frying pan over medium heat and brown the zucchini. Remove and set aside.

Sauté the bread crumbs in the same pan with 2 tablespoons of oil, 1 tablespoon of butter, and the garlic for 5 minutes. Remove and set aside.

Sauté the shallots and carrots in the remaining oil over medium heat until lightly browned. Add the asparagus and cream and cook for 10 minutes. Season with the salt.

Line a baking dish with a layer of the zucchini strips. Cover with a layer of the asparagus mixture and sprinkle with the bread crumbs and Parmesan. Repeat until all the ingredients are in the dish, finishing with a layer of bread crumbs and Parmesan. Dot with the remaining butter.

Bake until browned, 15–20 minutes. Serve hot.

1/3 cup (90 ml) extra-virgin olive oil

1½ lb (750 g) zucchini (courgettes), cut into thin strips lengthwise

1¾ cups (100 g) fresh bread crumbs

2 tablespoons butter, cut up

1 clove garlic, finely chopped

5 shallots, coarsely chopped

2 carrots, cut into small cubes

8 oz (250 g) asparagus tips, finely chopped

¾ cup (180 ml) heavy (double) cream

Salt

1 cup (125 g) freshly grated Parmesan cheese

SERVES 6–8

PREPARATION 15 min

COOKING 25–30 min

DIFFICULTY level 1

Baked Peppers

Preheat the oven to 400°F (200°C/gas 6).

Place the bell peppers in a large baking dish. Sprinkle with the onions, olives, and capers. Drizzle with the oil and season with salt.

Bake until the bell peppers are tender, 25–30 minutes.

Sprinkle with the oregano and serve hot.

3 lb (1.5 kg) red bell peppers (capsicums), seeded, cored, and cut into large pieces
1½ lb (750 g) onions, thickly sliced
20 green olives, pitted
2 tablespoons salt-cured capers, rinsed
⅓ cup (90 ml) extra-virgin olive oil
Salt
1 teaspoon dried oregano

Spinach Soufflés
with white wine sauce

Place the bread in a medium bowl and pour the milk over the top. Let stand until the milk has been absorbed, about 15 minutes.

Rinse the spinach under cold running water. Do not drain but place in a saucepan and cook, with just the water clinging to its leaves, for 3 minutes. Drain, press out excess moisture, chop coarsely, and set aside.

Melt 3 tablespoons of butter in a large frying pan and sauté the spinach.

Transfer a third of the spinach to a food processor. Add the soaked bread, Parmesan, eggs, almonds, remaining butter, and nutmeg. Season with salt and pepper. Process until very finely chopped.

Preheat the oven to 375°F (190°C/gas 5). Butter six small pudding molds or ramekins.

Spoon the chopped spinach mixture into the bottom and up the sides of the molds, pressing it firmly with the back of a spoon. Fill the center of the molds with the whole spinach leaves. Sprinkle with the carrots and cover with the remaining spinach leaves.

Half fill a large roasting pan with hot water and place the molds in the waterbath. Bake for 50 minutes.

Remove the molds from the waterbath and set aside for 10 minutes. Carefully invert the molds and turn the spinach soufflés onto serving plates.

White Wine Sauce: Bring the wine to a boil with the shallot. Simmer until the wine has reduced by half. Stir in the cream and bring to a boil once more. Simmer over low hwat for 5 minutes. Season with salt and pepper.

Spoon the sauce over the soufflés. Dust with the paprika and nutmeg and serve hot.

10 oz (300 g) firm-textured bread, crusts removed and cut into small cubes

3/4 cup (180 ml) milk

2 1/2 lb (1.25 kg) fresh spinach leaves, destalked

1/3 cup (90 g) butter

1/2 cup (60 g) freshly grated Parmesan cheese

2 eggs

2 oz (60 g) finely chopped almonds

1/8 teaspoon ground nutmeg

Salt and freshly ground black pepper

8 oz (250 g) carrots, cut in small cubes

White Wine Sauce

1 cup (250 ml) dry white wine

1 shallot, finely chopped

1 1/4 cups (300 ml) light (single) cream

Salt and freshly ground black pepper

1/4 teaspoon ground nutmeg

1/4 teaspoon paprika

Asparagus Soufflés

Preheat the oven to 325°F (170°C/gas 3). Butter six small soufflé dishes and sprinkle with semolina or bread crumbs.

Chop the asparagus stalks and set the tips aside. Stir the chopped asparagus, Parmesan, egg yolks, and nutmeg into the Béchamel.

Beat the egg whites and salt in a large bowl until stiff. Gently fold them into the asparagus mixture.

Spoon the mixture evenly into the prepared dishes. Bake until risen and golden, 20–25 minutes.

Garnish with the reserved asparagus tips and serve immediately.

12 asparagus stalks, boiled

1 tablespoon freshly grated Parmesan cheese

3 eggs, separated + 1 egg yolk

$1/8$ teaspoon freshly grated nutmeg

1 cup (250 ml) Béchamel Sauce (see page 47)

Potato Soufflé

Preheat the oven to 350°F (180°C/gas 4). Grease a 1-quart (1-liter) soufflé dish.

Cook the potatoes in a large pot of salted boiling water until tender, 20–25 minutes. Drain and mash in a large bowl using a potato ricer.

Add the cream and season with salt and pepper. Mix well. Add the egg yolks and mix well.

Beat the egg whites in a large bowl until stiff. Gently fold into the potato mixture.

Spoon the mixture into the soufflé dish. Bake for 15 minutes. Increase the oven temperature to 375°F (190°C/gas 5). Bake until well risen and golden brown, about 15 minutes. Serve at once.

1½ lb (750 g) starchy (baking) potatoes, peeled
⅓ cup (90 ml) heavy (double) cream
Salt and freshly ground black pepper
4 large eggs, separated

Baked Tomatoes

with risotto

Preheat the oven to 400°F (200°C/gas 6). Butter a shallow ovenproof dish into which the tomatoes will fit snugly.

Rinse and dry the tomatoes and cut a ½-inch (1-cm) thick slice from the stalk end. Set these "lids" aside. Discard the flesh and seeds.

Sauté the onion in 2 tablespoons of butter in a large frying pan over low heat until transparent. Add the rice and cook for 2 minutes, stirring constantly. Begin stirring in the stock, ½ cup (125 ml) at a time. Cook and stir until each addition has been absorbed, until the rice is tender, about 15–18 minutes. Stir in the Parmesan and season with salt and pepper.

Stuff the tomatoes with the risotto and top each one neatly with its lid.

Beat the eggs lightly in a bowl and dip the stuffed tomatoes into the beaten egg. Coat with the bread crumbs.

Place the tomatoes in a single layer, lid-side uppermost, in the prepared baking dish. Top each tomato with a flake of butter.

Bake until golden, 25–30 minutes.

Serve hot or at room temperature.

8 medium tomatoes
1 tablespoon very finely chopped onion
5 tablespoons butter
Scant 1 cup (180 g) risotto rice
2 cups (500 ml) boiling vegetable stock
½ cup (60 g) freshly grated Parmesan cheese
Salt and freshly ground black pepper
2 eggs
1 cup (125 g) fine dry bread crumbs

Vegetable Gratin

Preheat the oven to 350°F (180°C/gas 4). Butter a 12-inch (30-cm) baking dish.

Arrange half the zucchini in a layer in the prepared dish. Top with half the tomatoes. Sprinkle with half the garlic and basil. Season with salt and pepper and drizzle with the oil. Top with the remaining zucchini and cover with the remaining tomatoes. Sprinkle with the remaining garlic and basil.

Beat the egg and cream and season with salt and pepper. Pour over the vegetables.

Bake until the vegetables are tender, 50–60 minutes. Serve hot.

6 zucchini (courgettes), thinly sliced
6 tomatoes, finely chopped
6 cloves garlic, lightly crushed but whole
1 cup (60 g) finely chopped basil
    or parsley
Salt and freshly ground black pepper
¼ cup (60 ml) extra-virgin olive oil
1 egg
1 cup (250 ml) heavy (double) cream

Leek Gratin

Preheat the oven to 400°F (200°C/gas 6).

Cook the leeks in a large pot of salted, boiling water until just tender, 5–7 minutes. Drain well, pressing with a fork to remove excess water, and set aside.

Beat the cream and nutmeg in a large bowl until thickened. Season with salt and pepper. Spread 3 tablespoons of the cream in an ovenproof dish. Arrange the cooked leeks on top and pour the remaining cream over the top. Sprinkle with the Gruyère.

Bake until lightly browned and the cheese is bubbling, 25–30 minutes. Serve hot.

8–10 leeks, white parts only
1 cup (250 ml) heavy (double) cream
1 teaspoon freshly grated nutmeg
Salt and freshly ground black pepper
1 cup (120 g) g freshly grated Gruyère cheese

SERVES 4–6

PREPARATION 15 min

COOKING 1 h

DIFFICULTY level 1

Stuffed Potatoes

Preheat the oven to 350°F (180°C/gas 4). Bake the potatoes in the oven until tender, about 50 minutes.

Cut in half and scoop out the flesh. Mash in a bowl and add the nuts, raisins, and chilies. Mix well and stuff back into the potatoes.

Heat the oil in a large frying pan and sauté the onion and garlic until transparent. Add the tomatoes and spices and simmer over low heat until the oil separates, about 15 minutes. Add the yogurt, water, and salt and cook for 5 minutes. Add the potatoes and simmer for 5 more minutes. Serve hot.

6 medium potatoes

1 cup (100 g) mixed chopped cashew nuts and almonds

6 tablespoons raisins

2 chile peppers, thinly sliced

¼ cup (60 ml) extra-virgin olive oil

1 onion, finely chopped

2 cloves garlic, finely chopped

3 tomatoes, chopped

1 teaspooon cumin

1 teaspoon turmeric

⅓ cup (90 ml) plain yogurt

1 cup (250 ml) water

Salt

Potato Moussaka

Heat 2 tablespoons of oil in a large frying pan over medium heat. Sauté the onions for 8–10 minutes, or until lightly browned. Add the tofu and season with salt and pepper. Sprinkle with the parsley and nutmeg. Cook over low heat until the tofu has softened and browned, about 30 minutes.

Preheat the oven to 350°F (180°C/gas 4).

Heat the remaining oil in a large deep frying pan until very hot. Fry the potato slices, a few at a time, until softened, 5–7 minutes each batch.

Arrange a layer of potatoes in a baking pan and cover with a layer of tofu and tomatoes. Top with another layer of potatoes. Repeat until all the ingredients are used up, finishing with a layer of potatoes. Pour in the water and cover with aluminum foil.

Bake for 45 minutes. Remove the aluminum foil and bake until golden brown and crispy on top, 15–20 minutes. Serve hot.

1 cup (250 ml) extra-virgin olive oil
2 medium onions, finely chopped
8 oz (250 g) finely chopped dried tofu
Salt and freshly ground black pepper
1 tablespoon finely chopped parsley
$\frac{1}{8}$ teaspoon freshly ground nutmeg
1 cup (250 ml) water + more as needed
3 lb (1.5 kg) potatoes, peeled, and cut into $\frac{1}{2}$-inch (1-cm) slices
2 lb (1 kg) firm-ripe tomatoes, peeled and cut into cubes

Onion Gratin

SERVES 4–6

PREPARATION 30 min

COOKING 1 hour

DIFFICULTY level 1

Boil the potatoes in their skins in a pot of salted water until tender, about 25 minutes. Drain and cover to keep warm.

Place the onions, oil, half the butter, wine, water, stock cube, salt, and pepper in a saucepan, cover and simmer until the onions are soft, about 35 minutes.

Peel the potatoes, chop coarsely, and mash.

Heat the milk in a saucepan and add the potatoes and the remaining butter (reserving 1 tablespoon) to make a smooth purée. Remove from the heat and let cool for 10 minutes.

Combine the purée with the eggs, salt, and pepper. Stir in the Parmesan (reserving 2 tablespoons) and mix well.

Butter an ovenproof dish and spread with half the potato mixture in an even layer. Drain the cooked onions of any liquid and spread three-quarters of them over the potatoes. Sprinkle with the Gruyère and cover with the remaining potatoes. Top with the remaining onions. Sprinkle with bread crumbs and remaining Parmesan.

Bake in a preheated oven at 350°F (180°C/gas 4) for 25 minutes. Serve hot.

3 lb (1.5 kg) potatoes
6 large onions, sliced
1 tablespoon extra-virgin olive oil
$\frac{1}{2}$ cup (125 g) butter
1 cup (250 ml) dry white wine
$\frac{1}{2}$ cup (125 ml) water
1 vegetable stock cube
Salt and freshly ground black pepper
$1\frac{1}{4}$ cups (300 ml) milk
3 eggs, lightly beaten
1 cup (125 g) freshly grated Parmesan cheese
1 cup (125 g) freshly grated Gruyère cheese
2 tablespoons bread crumbs

SERVES 4–6

PREPARATION 10 min

COOKING 1 h

DIFFICULTY level 1

Spicy Potatoes

with cottage cheese

Preheat the oven to 350°F (180°C/gas 4).

Scrub the potatoes under cold running water. Pat dry and cut a slit in the top of each one. Prick with a fork, then wrap each potato in a piece of foil. Bake until tender, about 1 hour.

Place the cottage cheese in a heatproof bowl and set aside. Place the tomato paste, cumin, cilantro, red pepper flakes, salt, and pepper in another bowl.

Heat the oil in a small saucepan and sauté the onion and mustard seeds for 1 minute. Add the tomato paste mixture and water to the saucepan and mix well. Cook for 1 minute, then pour the spicy tomato mixture into the cottage cheese. Mix well.

When the potatoes are cooked, unwrap them and cut them open along the top. Divide the spicy cottage cheese equally among the six potatoes.

Rinse and dry the salad greens and place them on a serving dish. Arrange the potatoes on top and garnish the dish with the tomatoes and lemon. Serve hot.

6 medium potatoes

12 oz (350 g) cottage cheese

2 teaspoons tomato paste

1 teaspoon cumin seeds

1 teaspoon ground coriander

1 teaspoon red pepper flakes

Salt and freshly ground black pepper

1 tablespoon extra-virgin olive oil

1/2 teaspoon mixed onion and mustard seeds

3 tablespoons water

Mixed salad greens

2 tomatoes, cut in quarters, to garnish

Slices of fresh lemon, to garnish

Bell Peppers
stuffed with tabbouleh

Cook the bulgur in a large pot of salted, boiling water for 10 minutes. Turn off the heat and let swell in the water for 10 minutes. Drain and let cool completely.

Mix in the cucumber, tomatoes, and spring onions. Drizzle with the oil and season with salt and pepper. Mix in the raisins, lemon juice, mint, and parsley. Refrigerate for 2 hours.

Halve the peppers and remove the seeds and filaments. Fill with the tabbouleh. Garnish with the mint leaves and serve.

8 oz (250 g) bulgur
1 cucumber, peeled and diced
8 oz (250 g) cherry tomatoes, diced
2 spring onions, finely chopped
3 tablespoons extra-virgin olive oil
Salt and freshly ground black pepper
$1/3$ cup (60 g) golden raisins (sultanas)
Freshly squeezed juice of 2 lemons
2 tablespoons finely chopped mint
4 tablespoons finely chopped parsley
2 green bell peppers (capsicums)
2 red bell peppers (capsicums)
Mint leaves, to garnish

SERVES 4

PREPARATION 20 min + 1 h

COOKING 25–30 min

DIFFICULTY level 1

Baked Eggplant

Make several deep cuts in the tops of the eggplants. Place in a colander and sprinkle with salt. Let drain for 1 hour.

Preheat the oven to 350°F (180°C/gas 4).

Sauté the garlic and onions in 2 tablespoons of oil in a large frying pan over medium heat until lightly browned, 8–10 minutes. Season with salt. Add the tomatoes and simmer for 15 minutes.

Heat the remaining oil in a large frying pan until very hot. Fry the eggplants until the flesh has softened, 10–15 minutes.

Place the eggplants in a baking dish and fill with the onion mixture. Bake until tender, 25–30 minutes.

Sprinkle with the parsley and serve hot.

4 eggplants (aubergines), cut in half
1 tablespoon coarse sea salt
4 cloves garlic, finely chopped
4 onions, thinly sliced
1 cup (250 ml) extra-virgin olive oil
1 tablespoon finely chopped parsley
2 large firm-ripe tomatoes, finely chopped

SERVES 2–4

PREPARATION 25 min

COOKING 45–50 min

DIFFICULTY level I

Stuffed Zucchini

Preheat the oven to 350°F (180°C/gas 4). Oil a baking dish into which the zucchini will fit snugly.

Blanch the zucchini and onions in salted, boiling water for 5 minutes. Drain and use a spoon to scoop out the flesh from the center of the zucchini and onion halves.

Arrange the zucchini and onions in the prepared baking dish.

Filling: Chop the tofu finely and mix with the rice, zucchini and onion flesh, garlic, soy sauce, and salt.

Spoon the filling into the hollow-out zucchini and onions. Sprinkle with the bread crumbs and oregano and drizzle with the oil.

Bake until browned on top and the vegetables are tender, 40–45 minutes. Serve warm or at room temperature.

4 round zucchini (courgettes), tops cut off
2 onions, cut in half

Filling
4 oz (125 g) tofu (bean curd) or $\frac{1}{2}$ cup (100 g) chopped seitan (wheat curd)
$\frac{1}{2}$ cup (80 g) cooked rice
2 cloves garlic, finely chopped
I tablespoon soy sauce
$\frac{1}{2}$ teaspoon salt
3 tablespoons whole-wheat (wholemeal) bread crumbs
$\frac{1}{4}$ teaspoon dried oregano
I tablespoon vegetable oil

Baked Tomatoes
with parmesan, parsley, and garlic

Cut the tomatoes in half, remove the seeds with your fingers, sprinkle with a little salt, and place upside down in a colander for 20 minutes.

Preheat the oven to 350°F (180°C/gas 4).

Mix the garlic and parsley together in a bowl, add the bread crumbs and Parmesan, and, using a fork, work the oil in little by little. Season with salt and pepper.

Using a teaspoon, push the filling mixture into the tomato halves. Press it down with your fingers so that it sticks to the inside of the tomatoes (it will swell slightly in the oven and could overflow).

Place the filled tomatoes in a greased ovenproof dish and bake until tender, about 35 minutes.

Serve hot or at room temperature.

10 medium tomatoes
5 cloves garlic, finely chopped
1 cup (30 g) finely chopped parsley
$\frac{1}{2}$ cup (60 g) fine dry bread crumbs
$\frac{1}{2}$ cup (60 g) freshly grated Parmesan cheese
$\frac{1}{2}$ cup (125 ml) extra-virgin olive oil
Salt and freshly ground black pepper

Vegetables
en papillote

Preheat the oven to 350°F (180°C/gas 4).

Place all the vegetables in a large bowl. Add the garlic, rosemary, parsley, thyme, and oregano. Season with salt and pepper and add the oil. Mix well.

Line a roasting pan with a sheet of baking parchment, large enough to fold over all the vegetables.

Place the vegetable mixture in the baking parchment and close the paper over, folding to seal well. Secure the parcel with staples.

Bake until the vegetables are all tender, about 40 minutes. Remove from the oven and transfer to a large serving dish. Open the parchment package at the table and serve at once.

14 oz (400 g) Brussels sprouts, halved
1 small head broccoli, cut into florets
5 oz (150 g) cherry tomatoes
8 oz (200 g) baby carrots, tops removed
2 celery sticks, tough outer ridges removed and discarded, coarsely chopped
2 small leeks, sliced
2 cloves garlic, finely chopped
1 tablespoon finely chopped rosemary
1 tablespoon finely chopped parsley
1 tablespoon finely chopped thyme
1 tablespoon finely chopped oregano
Salt and freshly ground black pepper
5 tablespoons extra-virgin olive oil

FRIED VEGETABLES

Vegetable Samosas

Pastry: Sift the flour, baking powder, and salt into a large bowl. Mix in the ghee and enough milk to form a stiff dough.

Turn the dough out onto a lightly floured surface and knead until smooth. Roll out into a large rectangle and cut into 12 strips measuring about 3 x 8-inches (8 x 20-cm).

Filling: Cook the potato in a large pot of salted, boiling water until tender, 8–10 minutes. Drain and set aside.

Sauté the onion and tomato in the ghee in a large frying pan over medium heat until softened, 5 minutes. Mix in the garam masala, coriander powder, ginger, chile, and peas. Add the potato and cook for 5 minutes. Drizzle with the lemon juice.

Place a tablespoon of the filling in the center of each pastry strip. Brush the edges with water and fold over to form a triangle.

Heat the oil in a deep frying pan until very hot and fry the parcels in small batches until golden brown and crisp, 5–7 minutes each batch.

Remove with a slotted spoon and drain well on paper towels. Serve hot.

Variation: Replace the pastry in this recipe with 12 spring roll wrappers.

Pastry
1⅓ cups (200 g) all-purpose (plain) flour
½ teaspoon baking powder
⅛ teaspoon salt
1 tablespoon ghee (clarified butter)
3 tablespoons warm milk
   + more, as needed

Filling
1 potato, peeled and diced
1 small onion, finely chopped
1 tomato, chopped
2 tablespoons ghee (clarified butter)
1 tablespoon garam masala
1 teaspoon coriander powder
1 teaspoon grated fresh ginger
½ teaspoon chile powder
¾ cup (100 g) frozen peas
1 tablespoon freshly squeezed lemon juice
2 cups (500 ml) peanut oil, for frying

SERVES 4–6
PREPARATION 15 min
COOKING 40 min
DIFFICULTY level 2

Eggplant Fritters

Preheat the oven to 400°F (200°C/gas 6).

Cut the eggplants in half lengthwise and place them on a baking sheet. Bake until tender, 15–20 minutes. Let cool and scoop out the flesh with a spoon, mashing it coarsely with a fork.

Mix the eggplant, parsley, basil, garlic, Parmesan, eggs, salt and pepper, and enough bread crumbs to make a firm mixture. Shape into balls the size of walnuts. Roll in the bread crumbs.

Heat the oil in a large frying pan until very hot and fry in small batches until golden brown all over, 5–7 minutes each batch. Remove with a slotted spoon and drain on paper towels. Serve immediately.

2 eggplants (aubergines)
1 tablespoon finely chopped parsley
10 leaves fresh basil, torn
1 clove garlic, finely chopped
4 tablespoons freshly grated Parmesan cheese
2 eggs, lightly beaten
Salt and freshly ground black pepper
1 cup (125 g) fine dry bread crumbs
2 cups (500 ml) olive oil, for frying

Corn Fritters

Mix the flour, eggs, milk, corn, and Parmesan in a large bowl until well blended. Season with salt and pepper.

Heat the oil in a large frying pan until very hot and fry tablespoons of the corn mixture in small batches until golden brown, 5–7 minutes each batch.

Remove with a slotted spoon and drain on paper towels. Serve hot.

⅔ cup (100 g) all-purpose (plain) flour

2 eggs, lightly beaten

⅔ cup (150 ml) milk

3½ cups (350 g) canned corn (sweetcorn)

¾ cup (90 g) freshly grated Parmesan cheese

Salt and freshly ground black pepper

2 cups (500 ml) olive oil, for frying

Spinach Fritters

Cook the potatoes in their skins in a pot of salted, boiling water for about 25 minutes. Drain, peel, and mash.

Cook the spinach in a pot of salted, boiling water until tender (3–4 minutes if frozen, 8–10 minutes if fresh). Drain, cool under cold running water, squeeze out excess moisture, and chop finely.

Combine with the potatoes and mix well.

Put the eggs in a large bowl with the salt, pepper, potatoes, spinach, and Parmesan and blend with a fork until smooth.

Place a tablespoonful of the mixture in the palm of your hand. Press a cube of cheese into the center and close the mixture around it to make an oblong croquette. The cheese must be completely covered. Roll in the bread crumbs.

Heat the frying oil in a deep-fryer or frying pan until very hot.

Fry the fritters a few at a time, turning them in the oil so that they are golden brown all over. Remove with a slotted spoon and drain on paper towels. Repeat until all the croquettes are cooked.

Serve hot.

3 lb (1.5 kg) boiling potatoes

Salt and freshly ground black pepper

1 lb (500 g) fresh or 12 oz (350 g) frozen spinach

1 egg + 1 yolk, beaten

½ cup (60 g) freshly grated Parmesan cheese

5 oz (150 g) Taleggio or Fontina cheese (or other tasty, firm cheese), cut in small cubes

2 cups (250 g) fine dry bread crumbs

3 cups (750 ml) oil, for frying

Breaded Asparagus
with mint dip

Cook the asparagus in a large pot of salted, boiling water until almost tender, 5 minutes. Drain well.

Beat the eggs and Parmesan in a small bowl.

Heat the oil in a deep-fryer or large frying pan over medium heat.

Dip the asparagus tips in the beaten eggs and then in the bread crumbs, making sure they are well coated.

Fry the asparagus in small batches until golden brown, 3–4 minutes each batch. Drain on paper towels.

Beat the yogurt, mayonnaise, and mint in a small bowl. Season the asparagus with salt. Serve hot with the mint dip on the side.

1 lb (500 g) asparagus tips, (tough parts of the stems removed)
2 large eggs
3 tablespoons freshly grated Parmesan cheese
2 cups (500 ml) olive oil, for frying
1 cup (120 g) fine dry bread crumbs
1/2 cup (125 ml) plain yogurt
3/4 cup (180 ml) mayonnaise
1 tablespoon finely chopped mint
Salt

Herb Tempura

Place the flour in a large bowl and add the water. Beat with a whisk to make a smooth batter.

Heat the oil in a large frying pan over medium heat.

Dip the herbs in the batter and then drop them in the oil. Fry until golden brown, 2–3 minutes. Transfer to a layer of paper towels using a slotted spoon and let drain.

Arrange the herb tempura on a serving dish and sprinkle with salt. Serve hot.

1 cup (150 g) all-purpose (plain) flour
$1/3$ cup (90 ml) sparkling mineral water
1 cup (250 ml) sunflower oil, for frying
24 sage leaves
24 wild garlic leaves
16 sprigs of parsley
12 large basil leaves
Salt

Fried Sage Leaves

Rinse the sage leaves under cold running water, then pat dry with paper towels. Dredge the leaves in the flour. Dip in the egg and coat well with the bread crumbs.

Heat the oil in a large frying pan until very hot (test by dropping a leaf into the oil. If ready, it will sizzle sharply) and add half the leaves. They will turn golden brown almost immediately. Turn them once, then scoop them out with a slotted spoon. Drain on paper towels. Cook the remaining leaves.

Season with salt and serve hot.

40 large fresh sage leaves

2 tablespoons all-purpose (plain) flour

1 large egg, beaten until foamy with a pinch of salt

1½ cups (180 g) fine dry bread crumbs

2 cups (500 ml) sunflower oil, for frying

Salt

Zucchini Flowers

Rinse the flowers carefully under cold running water. Trim the stalks and dry the flowers carefully with paper towels.

Mix the Parmesan and bread crumbs in a large bowl. Add the parsley, 1 egg, and salt and pepper.

Use this mixture to carefully stuff the flowers.

Beat the remaining eggs in a small bowl. Place the flour in another small bowl and dip the stuffed flowers first in the flour and then in the egg.

Heat the oil in a large frying pan until very hot. Fry the flowers in small batches until golden, 5–7 minutes each batch. Remove with a slotted spoon and drain on paper towels.

Season with salt and serve hot.

20 fresh zucchini (courgette) flowers
6 tablespoons freshly grated Parmesan cheese
1 cup (125 g) fine dry bread crumbs
1 tablespoon finely chopped parsley
3 eggs
Salt and freshly ground black pepper
1 cup (150 g) all-purpose (plain) flour
1–2 cups (250–500 ml) olive oil, for frying

Tomato Croquettes

Blanch the tomatoes in boiling water for 1 minute. Drain and slip off the skins. Remove the seeds, chop coarsely, and let drain.

Mix the ricotta and egg yolks in a large bowl until smooth. Add the tomatoes, parsley, nutmeg, salt, and pepper and mix well. Form the mixture into croquettes of about 2 inches (5-cm) long and 1 inch (2.5-cm) thick. The mixture should be firm; if it is too runny, add 1–2 tablespoons dry bread crumbs or freshly grated Parmesan cheese.

Dredge the croquettes in the flour, dip them in the egg, and roll in the bread crumbs.

Heat the oil in a large frying pan until very hot. Fry the croquettes in small batches until golden brown, about 10 minutes. each batch

Remove with a slotted spoon and drain well on paper towels. Serve hot.

1 lb (500 g) ripe tomatoes
10 oz (300 g) ricotta cheese, drained and crumbled
2 eggs, beaten until foamy, + 2 egg yolks
2 tablespoons finely chopped parsley
1/4 teaspoon freshly grated nutmeg
Salt and freshly ground black pepper
1 cup (150 g) all-purpose (plain) flour
1 cup (125 g) fine dry bread crumbs
2 cups (500 ml) olive oil, for frying

Fried Vegetables

Cut the zucchini in half crosswise and cut each half in quarters lengthwise. Cut the eggplants in ¼-inch (5-mm) thick slices and cut each slice in halves or quarters (depending on how big they are).

Trim the stems of the zucchini flowers and rinse carefully. Drain on paper towels.

Heat the oil in a large frying pan until very hot.

Dredge the vegetables in the flour, then dip them in the egg.

Fry the vegetables in small batches until golden brown, 5–7 minutes each batch. Remove with a slotted spoon and drain well on paper towels. Season with salt and serve hot.

6 medium zucchini (courgettes)
2 large eggplants (aubergines)
12 large zucchini (courgette) flowers
2 cups (300 g) all-purpose (plain) flour
4 eggs, lightly beaten
3 cups (750 ml) olive oil, for frying
Salt

Cheese Fritters

Place three egg whites in a medium bowl with a pinch of salt and beat until stiff peaks form. Fold in both cheeses. Add half the flour. Season with salt and pepper.

Shape the mixture into balls the size of walnuts.

Beat the remaining egg and yolk. Dip the fritters in the egg. Roll in the remaining flour and then in the bread crumbs.

Heat the oil in a deep-fryer or frying pan to very hot.

Fry the fritters in batches until golden brown all over. Remove with a slotted spoon and drain on paper towels. Serve hot.

2 eggs + 2 egg whites
Salt and freshly ground white pepper
8 oz (250 g) freshly grated Gruyère or Cheddar cheese
6 tablespoons freshly grated Parmesan cheese
2/3 cup (100 g) all-purpose (plain) flour
1 cup (150 g) fine dry bread crumbs
2 cups (500 ml) olive oil, for frying

Ricotta Fritters

Mix together the ricotta, fresh bread crumbs, Parmesan, parsley, and salt in a large bowl.

Shape the mixture into balls the size of walnuts. Roll the balls in the dry bread crumbs.

Heat the oil in a deep-fryer or frying pan to very hot. Fry the fritters in batches until golden brown all over. Remove with a slotted spoon and drain on paper towels. Serve hot.

1½ cups (375 g) ricotta cheese, drained
2½ cups (200 g) fresh bread crumbs
½ cup (60 g) freshly grated Parmesan cheese
1 tablespoon finely chopped parsley
Salt
½ cup (60 g) fine dry bread crumbs
2 cups (500 ml) olive oil, for frying

Fried Cauliflower
with vinegar marinade

Cook the cauliflower florets in a pot of salted, boiling water until just tender, 4–5 minutes. Drain well, and place on a clean tea towel to dry.

Combine the beaten eggs with the beer.

Heat the frying oil in a large frying pan until very hot.

Dredge the florets in the flour, shaking off the excess.

When the oil is hot, dip about 10 florets in the egg mixture. Coat well and transfer to the pan. Turn a couple of times with two forks or tongs. Fry until golden brown all over, about 10 minutes. Scoop out with a slotted spoon and drain on paper towels. Repeat with the remaining cauliflower.

To prepare the marinade, place the vinegar in a small saucepan with the spring onions. Simmer for 5–6 minutes, then add the thyme, and remove from the heat. Pour into a serving bowl.

Serve the marinade and cauliflower florets hot.

1 small cauliflower (about 1 lb/500 g), divided into florets
Salt and freshly ground black pepper
3 eggs, beaten until foamy
$\frac{1}{4}$ cup (60 ml) beer
2 cups (500 ml) oil, for frying
1 cup (150 g) all-purpose (plain) flour
1 cup (250 ml) white wine vinegar
2 spring onions, finely chopped
1 teaspoon finely chopped fresh or $\frac{1}{2}$ teaspoon dry thyme

Mozzarella Fritters

Prepare the pizza dough.

Blanch the tomatoes in boiling water for 2 minutes. Drain and peel. Chop the tomatoes, discarding the seeds.

Place the tomatoes, mozzarella, and oregano in a bowl. Season with salt and pepper, mix well.

Roll out the dough on a lightly floured work surface to ¼ inch (5 mm) thick. Cut it into 4-inch (10-cm) disks using a large glass or cookie cutter.

Place a little of the filling in the center of each disk. Moisten the edges of the dough and fold it in half to cover the filling. Pinch the edges together to seal.

Heat the oil in a deep-fryer or frying pan to very hot. Fry the fritters in batches until puffed and golden brown, 7–8 minutes each batch. Remove with a slotted spoon and drain on paper towels. Serve hot.

1 quantity pizza dough (see pages 72–73)
14 oz (400 g) firm ripe tomatoes
6 oz (180 g) fresh mozzarella cheese, cut into small cubes
1 teaspoon dried oregano
Salt and freshly ground black pepper
2 cups (500 ml) oil, for frying

SERVES 6

PREPARATION 20 min

COOKING 30 min

DIFFICULTY level 2

Vegetarian
spring rolls

Heat the peanut oil in a wok and stir-fry the celery for 3 minutes. Add the bean sprouts, black mushrooms, carrots, and bamboo shoots and stir-fry for 5 minutes. Add the soy sauce, sesame oil, salt, and sugar.

Divide the filling into 12 equal portions. Wrap one portion of filling in each of the spring roll wrappers.

Mix the flour and water to form a smooth paste. Use the paste to seal the spring rolls.

Heat the oil to very hot in a large frying pan and fry the spring rolls in two batches until golden brown, about 10 minutes each batch. Remove with a slotted spoon and drain on paper towels. Serve immediately.

2 tablespoons peanut oil
1 stalk celery, finely chopped
4 oz (125 g) mung bean sprouts
3 oz (90 g) dried black Chinese mushrooms, cut in very thin strips
2 oz (60 g) carrots, cut in very thin strips
2 oz (60 g) bamboo shoots
1 teaspoon soy sauce
1 teaspoon sesame oil
$1/2$ teaspoon salt
$1/2$ teaspoon sugar
12 spring roll wrappers
1 tablespoon all-purpose (plain) flour
1 tablespoon water
1 quart (1 liter) oil, for frying

Peanut Fritters

Place the peanuts in a wok and dry-fry over low heat for 5 minutes. Rub them to remove the skins and chop coarsely.

Process the coriander seeds, ginger, garlic, red pepper flakes, salt, and turmeric in a food processor or blender until smooth.

Sift both flours into a large bowl. Mix in the spice mixture and coconut milk, blending well. Add the peanuts.

Heat the oil in a wok until very hot and fry tablespoons of batter in small batches until golden brown. Remove with a slotted spoon and drain well on paper towels. Serve hot.

- 1¼ cups (200 g) raw peanuts
- 1 teaspoon coriander seeds
- 2 teaspoons finely chopped ginger
- 2 cloves garlic
- 1 teaspoon red pepper flakes (or 2 crumbled dried chilies)
- 1 teaspoon salt
- ½ teaspoon ground turmeric
- 1 cup (150 g) rice flour
- ⅔ cup (100 g) all-purpose (plain flour)
- 1 cup (250 ml) coconut milk
- 2 cups (500 ml) oil, for frying

BEANS
& LENTILS

SERVES 4

PREPARATION 10 min + time to soak beans

COOKING 2 h

DIFFICULTY level 1

Baked Beans

with tomatoes and herbs

Cook the beans in a large pan of salted water until tender, about 1 hour. Drain well.

Preheat the oven to 400°F (200°C/gas 6).

Place the beans in a large baking dish. Mix in the tomatoes, garlic, herbs, and oil. Season with salt and pepper.

Bake for 1 hour. Serve hot.

8 oz (250 g) cannellini or white kidney beans, soaked overnight and drained

1 lb (500 g) peeled and chopped tomatoes

2 cloves garlic, lightly crushed but whole

2 tablespoons finely chopped mixed fresh herbs (such as thyme, basil, and oregano)

1/3 cup (90 ml) extra-virgin olive oil

Salt and freshly ground black pepper

Soy Bean Balls

Cook the soy beans in a large pot of salted water until tender, about 3 hours. Drain and let cool.

Preheat the oven to 400°F (200°C/gas 6). Oil a baking dish.

Sauté half the onion in 2 tablespoons of oil in a large frying pan until softened, 3–4 minutes. Stir in the tomatoes and season with salt and pepper. Add the flour mixture, thyme, bay leaf, wine, and stock. Simmer over medium-low heat for 20 minutes.

Sauté the eggplant in the remaining oil in a medium frying pan until golden. Remove from the pan and sauté the bell pepper and remaining onion in the same oil until softened.

Transfer the bell pepper mixture to a large bowl. Mix in the soy beans, eggplant, garlic, bread crumbs, Parmesan, and eggs. Season with salt and pepper. Form the mixture into rissoles.

Arrange the rissoles in the prepared baking dish. Bake for 10 minutes.

Pour over half the sauce and bake until the rissoles are golden, about 15 minutes. Serve hot with the remaining sauce.

$3\frac{1}{2}$ oz (100 g) yellow soy beans, soaked overnight and drained

1 onion, chopped

$\frac{1}{3}$ cup (90 ml) extra-virgin olive oil

4 large tomatoes, peeled and chopped

Salt and freshly ground black pepper

1 tablespoon whole-wheat (wholemeal) flour mixed in 2 tablespoons water

2 sprigs thyme

1 bay leaf

3 tablespoons dry red wine

$1\frac{1}{4}$ cups (300 ml) vegetable stock

1 eggplant (aubergine), diced

1 red bell pepper (capsicum), seeded, cored, and finely chopped

1 clove garlic, finely chopped

$3\frac{1}{2}$ cups (200 g) fresh bread crumbs

$1\frac{1}{4}$ cups (150 g) freshly grated Parmesan cheese

2 eggs, lightly beaten

Lentil Curry

Cook the lentils, onions, tomatoes, curry leaves, turmeric, water, and salt in a large saucepan over medium heat for 15–20 minutes.

Add the vegetables that take longer to cook, such as carrots and potatoes, along with the tamarind pulp and liquid, coconut, and sugar. Simmer until the vegetables are softening and the lentils have broken down, about 15 minutes. Add the remaining vegetables and cilantro and simmer for 10 minutes.

Heat the oil in a small saucepan. Sauté the mustard seed and chilies until aromatic, 1–2 minutes. Add to the vegetable curry, stir well, and cook for 2 minutes. Serve hot.

8 oz (250 g) small yellow lentils

2 onions, finely sliced

2 tomatoes, chopped

2 sprigs curry leaves

$\frac{1}{2}$ teaspoon ground turmeric

1 quart (1 liter) water

1 teaspoon salt

$1\frac{3}{4}$ lb (800 g) mixed vegetables, such as carrots, potatoes, eggplant (aubergines), cauliflower, and green beans, cut into small pieces

$\frac{1}{2}$ cup (90 g) tamarind pulp soaked in 1 cup (250 ml) hot water, strained, liquid reserved

1 cup (100 g) freshly grated coconut blended with $\frac{1}{3}$ cup (90 ml) water

$\frac{1}{2}$ teaspoon sugar

1 tablespoon finely chopped cilantro (coriander)

2 tablespoons peanut oil

1 teaspoon mustard seeds

3–4 dried red chile peppers, crumbled

Curried Dal Balls

Process the dal, fresh chilies, and turmeric in a food processor until a paste has formed. Season with salt and pepper and add the carrots. Shape into balls or oblongs 1-inch (2.5-cm) in diameter and arrange in a steamer lightly greased with oil. Steam for 10 minutes then set aside.

Grind the dried chilies and fenugreek to a paste with a pestle and mortar. Stir the ground spices into the tamarind water in a medium bowl.

Heat the oil in a small saucepan over medium heat. Add the cumin seeds, mustard seeds, and curry leaves and cook until aromatic. Pour in the tamarind mixture and bring to a boil. Simmer for 20 minutes.

Add the dal balls and simmer for 10 minutes more. Serve hot.

10 oz (300 g) Urad (split black lentils), black skins removed, soaked in cold water for 3 hours and drained

2 small red chile peppers, finely chopped

1/2 teaspoon ground turmeric

Salt and freshly ground black pepper

2 carrots, finely grated

6 dried red chile peppers, crumbled

3/4 teaspoon ground fenugreek

1/2 cup (90 g) tamarind pulp soaked in 1 quart (1 liter) hot water, strained, liquid reserved

2 tablespoons peanut oil

1 teaspoon cumin seeds

1/2 teaspoon mustard seeds

6 curry leaves

Quick Bean Chile

Heat the oil and butter in a large saucepan over medium heat. Add the onions, chile peppers, ginger, cardamom, ground coriander, and garlic and sauté for 7–8 minutes.

Pour in tomato and add the beans and bay leaf. Mix well and simmer over medium heat for 15 minutes. Stir often to stop the mixture sticking to the pan. Season with salt and pepper.

Transfer to a serving dish and garnish with parsley and cilantro. Serve hot.

3 tablespoons extra-virgin olive oil

2 tablespoons butter

1 tablespoon grated ginger

Seeds from 4 cardamom pods

1 tablespoon ground coriander

5 cloves garlic, sliced

2 onions, finely chopped

2 fresh red chile peppers, sliced

1 cup (250 ml) tomato passata

2 cups (250 g) canned garbanzo beans (chickpeas), drained

2 cups (250 g) red kidney beans

2 cups (200 g) pinto beans, drained

1 bay leaf

Salt and freshly ground black pepper

1 tablespoon finely chopped parsley

1 teaspoon finely chopped cilantro (coriander)

SERVES 4

PREPARATION 15 min

COOKING 1 h

DIFFICULTY level 2

Lentils and Rice
with tomato sauce

Cover the lentils with boiling water in a large saucepan. Simmer over low heat until the lentils are well cooked, about 30 minutes.

Cook the rice in a large pot of salted, boiling water until tender, about 15 minutes.

Tomato Sauce: Sauté the onion and garlic in the oil in a large saucepan over medium heat for 5 minutes. Stir in the tomatoes and cook until the tomatoes have reduced, 10–15 minutes. Add the water and vinegar and simmer for 5–10 minutes. Season with salt and pepper.

Spoon a layer of lentils onto each of four serving dishes. Add a layer of rice and repeat the layering until all the rice and lentils are used. Spoon the tomato sauce over the top. Serve hot.

1½ cups (350 g) yellow lentils
1¼ cups (250 g) short-grain rice

Tomato Sauce
1 large onion, finely sliced
1 clove garlic, finely chopped
¼ cup (60 ml) extra-virgin olive oil
2 lb (1 kg) tomatoes, peeled and finely chopped
⅔ cup (150 ml) water
2 tablespoons vinegar
Salt and freshly ground black pepper

SERVES 6–8

PREPARATION 20 min + time to soak beans

COOKING 1 h 30 min

DIFFICULTY level 1

Black Beans
in mango sauce

Place the beans in a large saucepan with enough water to cover and bring to a boil over low heat. Remove from the heat and let soak for 2 hours. Drain.

Pour in the boiling water and add the bay leaves. Bring to a boil and simmer over low heat for 1 hour 15 minutes, or until the beans are tender. Drain and discard the bay leaves. Let cool completely.

Mix the beans, mango, lemon and orange juices, maple syrup, and cilantro in a large bowl. Season with salt and pepper. Drizzle with the lime juice and refrigerate until ready to serve.

Serve with freshly made tortillas.

- 8 oz (250 g) dried black beans, soaked overnight and drained
- 1 quart (1 liter) boiling water
- 4 bay leaves
- 10 oz (300 g mango), peeled and cut into cubes
- 1 tablespoon freshly squeezed lemon juice
- 1 tablespoon freshly squeezed orange juice
- 1 tablespoon maple syrup
- 3 tablespoons finely chopped cilantro (coriander)
- Salt and freshly ground black pepper
- 1 tablespoon freshly squeezed lime juice
- Wheat tortillas, to serve

SERVES 6–8

PREPARATION 30 min + time to soak

COOKING 20-30 min

DIFFICULTY level 1

Houmous

Soak the garbanzo beans in a large bowl of water overnight. Rinse well and cook over low heat until tender, about 50 minutes.

Place the garbanzo beans (reserving a few to garnish), tahini, lemon juice, garlic, salt, and pepper in a blender or food processor and chop finely. Add enough of the water to obtain a smooth and creamy dip.

Garnish with the parsley and reserved garbanzo beans and serve.

1 lb (500 g) garbanzo beans (chickpeas)
$\frac{1}{4}$ cup (60 ml) tahini (sesame seed paste)
2 tablespoons freshly squeezed lemon juice
2 cloves garlic, finely chopped
Salt and freshly ground black pepper
$\frac{3}{4}$ cup (180 ml) water
Sprig of parsley, to garnish

Lentil Toasts

Place the lentils in a large saucepan with the stock. Bring to a boil over medium heat and simmer for 30 minutes, or until tender. Drain and set aside.

Sauté the onion in 2 tablespoons of oil in a large saucepan until softened, 5 minutes. Season with salt. Add the tomatoes and lentils and sauté for 3 minutes. Add the spinach and cook until the spinach is wilted, 3–4 minutes.

Beat the remaining oil and vinegar in a small bowl. Season with salt and pepper. Rub the toast all over with the garlic.

Arrange the toast on serving dishes and spoon the lentil and spinach mixture over the top. Drizzle with the remaining oil and vinegar and serve.

7 oz (200 g) Puy lentils
$2^{2}/_{3}$ cups (650 ml) vegetable stock
1 large onion, coarsely chopped
$^{1}/_{4}$ cup (60 ml) extra-virgin olive oil
Salt and freshly ground black pepper
4 tomatoes, peeled and coarsely chopped
1 lb (500 g) spinach, tough stems removed, chopped
2 tablespoons balsamic vinegar
8 slices toasted bread, crusts removed
1 clove garlic, peeled

SERVES 6–8

PREPARATION 25 min + 26 h to soak and rest

COOKING 25 min

DIFFICULTY level 2

Falafel

Soak the garbanzo beans in a large bowl of water for 24 hours.

Drain and rinse well. Place the garbanzo beans, onion, garlic, potato, and parsley in a food processor and chop coarsely. Add the coriander, oregano, cumin, salt, pepper, flour, and baking powder and process until well mixed. Set aside to rest for 2 hours.

Heat the oil in a large frying pan until very hot. Scoop out tablespoons of the mixture and shape into slightly flattened patties. Fry the falafel in batches of 4–5 until golden brown. Drain on paper towels.

Serve the falafel hot or warm as a starter or snack or use them to fill pita bread with salad greens and sliced tomatoes.

1 lb (500 g) garbanzo beans (chickpeas)
1 medium onion
2–3 cloves garlic, finely chopped
1 medium potato
1 small bunch parsley
1 teaspoon ground coriander
1 teaspoon cumin seeds
1 teaspoon dried oregano
1 teaspoon salt
1 teaspoon freshly ground white pepper
3 tablespoons all-purpose (plain) flour
2 teaspoons baking powder
2 cups (500 ml) oil, for frying

Crostini
with garbanzo bean purée

Soak the garbanzo beans overnight in a large bowl of cold water with the baking soda. Drain and rinse well.

Transfer to a pressure cooker with the ½ cup (125 ml) of water and cook for 10 minutes. Open the pressure cooker and add the sesame oil, lemon juice, and a pinch of salt. Top up the water if necessary. Close and cook for 10 minutes more. (If you do not have a pressure cooker, cook the beans in a large pan of lightly salted water until tender, about 1 hour. Drain the beans and add the sesame oil, lemon juice, and a pinch of salt.)

Chop the garbanzo beans in a food processor until smooth. Add the garlic, paprika, and parsley and mix well.

Spread the garbanzo bean mixture over the toast and serve.

- 8 oz (250 g) dried garbanzo beans (chickpeas)
- 1 teaspoon baking soda (bicarbonate of soda)
- ¼ cup (60 ml) sesame oil
- Freshly squeezed juice of 2 lemons
- Salt
- 1 clove garlic, finely chopped
- ⅛ teaspoon mild paprika
- 1 tablespoon finely chopped parsley
- 10–12 slices whole-wheat (wholemeal bread), toasted

RICE & GRAINS

SERVES 4

PREPARATION 15 min

COOKING 40 min

DIFFICULTY level 1

Risotto
with tomato and fresh basil

Melt 2 tablespoons of the butter in a large saucepan over medium heat. Add the onion and sauté until transparent, 3–4 minutes. Add the tomatoes and mix well. Cook until the tomatoes have broken down and the mixture is slightly thickened, about 20 minutes.

Melt 2 tablespoons of the remaining butter in a large frying pan over medium heat. Add the rice and sauté for 2 minutes. Pour in the wine and and cook until it evaporates. Stir in the tomato sauce and basil. Begin adding the stock, 1/2 cup (125 ml) at a time, cooking and stirring until each addition has been absorbed and the rice is tender, 15–18 minutes.

Stir in the remaining butter and the Parmesan. Season with salt and pepper.

Remove from the heat and let rest for 1 minute. Garnish with the extra basil and serve hot.

1/3 cup (90 g) butter
1 small onion, finely chopped
2 cups (500 g) peeled and chopped tomatoes
1 3/4 cups (350 g) risotto rice
1/3 cup (90 ml) dry white wine
3 cups (750 ml) boiling vegetable stock (homemade or bouillon cube)
20 basil leaves, torn + extra, to garnish
1/4 cup (30 g) freshly grated Parmesan cheese
Salt and freshly ground black pepper

Risotto
with pear and goat cheese

Preheat the oven to 350°F (180°C/gas 4).

Cut one of the pears in quarters and remove the core. Slice very thinly and place the slices on a baking sheet lined with baking parchment. Bake, turning from time to time, until the slices have dried out, 15–20 minutes. Set aside. Core and chop the remaining pears.

Place the wine in a small saucepan and bring to a boil over low heat. Simmer for 10 minutes.

Melt the butter in a large frying pan over medium heat. Add the shallot and sauté until transparent, 3–4 minutes.

Add the rice and sauté for 2 minutes. Pour in the hot wine and cook until it evaporates, 2–3 minutes. Add ½ cup (125 ml) of the stock and cook until it is absorbed. Add the chopped pears and mix well. Keep adding the stock, ½ cup (125 ml) at a time, cooking and stirring until each addition has been absorbed and the rice is tender, 15–18 minutes.

Season with salt and pepper. Remove from the heat. Stir in the goat cheese and ginger. Cover and let rest for 2 minutes.

Top with the baked pears. Garnish with marjoram and serve hot.

3 large ripe pears
½ cup (125 ml) dry white wine
2 tablespoons butter
1 shallot, finely chopped
1¾ cups (350 g) risotto rice
3 cups (750 ml) vegetable stock,
     (homemade or bouillon cube), boiling
Salt and freshly ground black pepper
8 oz (250 g) fresh creamy goat cheese
2 tablespoons chopped candied ginger
Fresh marjoram, to garnish

SERVES 4–6

PREPARATION 10 min

COOKING 15 min

DIFFICULTY level 1

Brown Rice
with sage and soy sauce

Cook the rice in a large pot of salted, boiling water until tender, about 15 minutes. Drain well and transfer to a large bowl.

Meanwhile, sauté the garlic and sage in the oil in a small frying pan over medium heat until the garlic is pale gold. Stir in the soy sauce.

Drizzle the dressing over the rice and mix well. Garnish with the sage and serve hot.

- 1½ cups (300 g) quick-cooking parboiled brown rice
- 2 cloves garlic, thinly sliced
- 12 leaves sage, finely chopped + extra, to garnish
- ⅓ cup (90 ml) extra-virgin olive oil
- 2 tablespoons dark soy sauce

SERVES 4

PREPARATION 10 min

COOKING 25 min

DIFFICULTY level 1

Risotto
with gorgonzola

Sauté the onion in the butter in a large frying pan over medium heat until softened, 3–4 minutes. Add the rice and cook for 2 minutes, stirring constantly.

Stir in the wine and when this has been absorbed, begin stirring in the stock, ½ cup (125 ml) at a time. Cook and stir until each addition has been absorbed, until the rice is tender, about 15–18 minutes.

Stir in the Gorgonzola. Sprinkle with the cilantro and serve hot.

1 large onion, finely chopped

2 tablespoons butter

1½ cups (300 g) risotto rice

⅓ cup (90 ml) dry white wine

1 quart (1 liter) vegetable stock (homemade or bouillon cube)

4 oz (125 g) creamy Gorgonzola cheese, cut into cubes

2 tablespoons finely chopped cilantro (coriander)

Vegetable Risotto
with smoked cheese

Sauté the shallots in half the butter and the oil in a large frying pan over medium heat until the shallot has softened, 3–4 minutes. Add the rice and cook for 2 minutes, stirring constantly. Stir in the wine and when this has been absorbed add the vegetables.

Begin stirring in the stock, ½ cup (125 ml) at a time. Cook and stir until each addition has been absorbed, until the rice is tender, about 15–18 minutes.

Remove from the heat and stir in the Provola cubes, the remaining butter, and parsley. Season with salt and pepper. Arrange the sliced Provola on top of the risotto and serve hot.

2 shallots, finely chopped
⅓ cup (90 g) butter
2 tablespoons extra-virgin olive oil
2 cups (400 g) risotto rice
⅓ cup (90 ml) dry white wine
1 quart (1 liter) vegetable stock (homemade or bouillon cube)
8 oz (250 g) mixed frozen vegetables
3 oz (90 g) smoked Provola or other mild smoked cheese, cut into cubes
1 tablespoon finely chopped parsley
Salt and freshly ground black pepper
2 oz (60 g) smoked Provola or other mild smoked cheese, thinly sliced

SERVES 4–6

PREPARATION 20 min

COOKING 40 min

DIFFICULTY level I

Risotto
with spring vegetables

Clean the artichokes by pulling the tough outer leaves down and snapping them off. Cut off the top third of the leaves and trim the stalk. Cut in half and use a sharp knife to remove any fuzzy choke. Slice thinly and drizzle with the lemon juice.

Blanch the tomatoes in boiling water for 2 minutes. Drain and peel. Chop finely with a large knife.

Heat the oil and half the butter in a large frying pan over medium heat. Add the onion, celery, and parsley and sauté until tender, about 5 minutes. Add the carrot, potatoes, artichokes, and tomatoes to the pan and season with salt. Sauté for 2–3 minutes and then add a ½ cup (125 ml) of stock. Simmer over low heat until the potatoes and the carrots begin to soften, about 10 minutes. Add the peas, green beans, spinach, and asparagus. Add the rice and stir for 2 minutes.

Begin adding the stock, ½ cup (125 ml) at a time, cooking and stirring until each addition has been absorbed and the rice is tender, 15–18 minutes.

Remove from the heat and add the Parmesan and remaining butter. Season with pepper and serve hot.

2 artichokes

Freshly squeezed juice of 1 lemon

3 large ripe tomatoes

2 tablespoons extra-virgin olive oil

⅓ cup (90 g) butter

1 medium onion, finely chopped

1 stalk celery, finely chopped

4 tablespoons finely chopped parsley

1 large carrot, cut in small cubes

2 medium potatoes, peeled and cut in small cubes

Salt

1 quart (1 liter) boiling vegetable stock (homemade or bouillon cube)

2 cups (300 g) frozen peas

4 oz (125 g) green beans, coarsely chopped

5 oz (150 g) fresh spinach, coarsely chopped

8 oz (250 g) asparagus tips, coarsely chopped

2 cups (400 g) Italian risotto rice

¼ cup (30 g) freshly grated Parmesan cheese

Freshly ground black pepper

Green Paella

Wash the spinach and cook with just the water left clinging to its leaves until wilted, 5–7 minutes. Drain, squeezing out any excess moisture. Chop coarsely.

Sauté the onions and garlic in the oil in a large frying pan over medium heat until the garlic is pale gold, 3–4 minutes. Add the pine nuts and chile and cook for 2 minutes. Lower the heat and add the tomatoes and bell pepper. Cook for 6 minutes, stirring constantly. Add the rice and sauté for 2 minutes. Season with salt and pepper. Add the paprika, saffron water, and enough stock to cover the rice by about 1 inch (2.5 cm).

Bring to a boil and simmer until the rice is tender and almost all the liquid has evaporated, about 15 minutes. Stir occasionally during the cooking time to prevent the rice from sticking to the pan.

Add the spinach and peas and mix well. Simmer until the peas are cooked, about 5 minutes. Remove from the heat, cover, and let rest for 5 minutes. Garnish with the peppers and serve.

1 lb (500 g) spinach

2 onions, sliced

3 cloves garlic, finely chopped

1/3 cup (90 ml) extra-virgin olive oil

2 tablespoons pine nuts

1 dried red chile pepper, crumbled

8 oz (250 g) tomatoes, peeled and chopped

1 large green bell pepper (capsicum), seeded, cored, and sliced

1 1/4 cups (250 g) short-grain rice

Salt and freshly ground black pepper

1 teaspoon sweet paprika

1/2 teaspoon saffron strands, soaked in boiling water for 15 minutes

3 cups (750 ml) vegetable stock

3/4 cup (90 g) frozen peas

7 oz (200 g) Spanish piquillo peppers, sliced (optional)

Spiced Couscous
with mushrooms

Bring the water to a boil in a large saucepan over medium heat.

Add 1 tablespoon of oil and 1 teaspoon of salt. Stir in the couscous and cumin and mix well. Remove from the heat, cover and let rest for 2 minutes. Add the remaining oil and return to the heat. Simmer for 3 minutes, stirring constantly with a fork to separate the grains.

Remove from the heat and add the garlic, mushrooms, tomatoes, pecorino, and marjoram. Season with salt and pepper. Sprinkle with the pine nuts.

Serve hot or at room temperature.

Generous 1⅓ cups (350 ml) water
5 tablespoons extra-virgin olive oil
Salt and freshly ground black pepper
2⅔ cups (400 g) precooked couscous
1 tablespoon cumin seeds
2 cloves garlic, finely chopped
8 oz (250 g) mushrooms, washed and thinly sliced
12 cherry tomatoes, cut in half
8 oz (250 g) Parmesan cheese, cut into flakes
2 tablespoons finely chopped marjoram
Generous ¼ cup (50 g) pine nuts, toasted

Couscous
with peas and asparagus

Place the couscous in a large bowl. Pour in the boiling water, cumin, salt, and 1 tablespoon of oil. Let stand for 10 minutes, or until the couscous has absorbed the water. Break up with a fork and drizzle with 1 tablespoon of oil.

Cook the asparagus, peas, and corn in a large pot of salted, boiling water until tender, 5–7 minutes. Drain well. Cut the asparagus into short lengths.

Beat together the lemon juice and the remaining oil. Season with salt and pepper. Drizzle the dressing over the couscous.

Mix the peas into the couscous and arrange the asparagus, baby corn, and lemon zest on top. Serve warm.

2 cups (300 g) precooked couscous
1 1/4 cups (300 ml) boiling water
Salt
1 teaspoon cumin seeds
5 tablespoons extra-virgin olive oil
Salt and freshly ground black pepper
8 oz (250 g) fresh or frozen tender asparagus tips
1 cup (150 g) frozen peas
5 oz (150 g) baby corn (sweetcorn)
Freshly squeezed juice of 1 lemon
Zest of 1 lemon, very finely sliced

Zucchini Wheat
with walnuts and parmesan

Soak the wheat in cold water for 12 hours. Drain and transfer to a large saucepan. Pour in enough hot water to cover the wheat with double the volume.

Bring to a boil and cook until tender, 1–2 hours.

Rinse the zucchini, pat them dry, and slice thinly. Grill on a hot griddle or grill pan for 30 seconds on each side.

Transfer to a bowl. Season with salt and pepper, and drizzle with 2 tablespoons of the oil. Sprinkle the parsley and mint over the top.

Drain the wheat thoroughly and set aside. Let cool.

Place the zucchini on a large serving dish and spoon the wheat over the top. Drizzle with the remaining oil and the lemon juice.

Add the toasted walnuts, Parmesan cheese and, if liked, a few more leaves of fresh mint.

10 oz (300 g) wheat berries
4 zucchini (courgettes)
Salt and freshly ground black pepper
20 walnuts, shelled, chopped, and toasted
2 tablespoons finely chopped parsley
1 tablespoon finely chopped mint
  + extra leaves to garnish
3 oz (100 g) Parmesan cheese, in thin flakes
1/3 cup (90 ml) extra-virgin olive oil
1 tablespoon freshly squeezed lemon juice

Bulgur Wheat
with walnuts

Soak the bulgur wheat in warm water for 15 minutes. Drain, squeezing out the excess water.

Chop the walnuts coarsely with 1 teaspoon of salt on a chopping board.

Mix the bulgur wheat, walnuts, onion, tomatoes, and mint in a large bowl. Drizzle with the oil. Refrigerate for 15 minutes.

Stir the garlic into the yogurt. Garnish the chilled dish with the mint and serve with the garlic-flavored yogurt.

2 cups (250 g) bulgur wheat
$2\frac{1}{3}$ cups (400 g) shelled walnuts
1 teaspoon salt
1 onion, finely chopped
16 cherry tomatoes, halved
2 tablespoons finely chopped mint
    + 1 sprig mint, to garnish
$\frac{1}{4}$ cup (60 ml) extra-virgin olive oil
2 cloves garlic, finely chopped
1 cup (250 ml) plain yogurt

Couscous
with mint and zucchini

Grill the zucchini in a hot grill pan until tender, 3–4 minutes. Transfer to a large bowl. Add 4 tablespoons of oil, the vinegar, shallots, cumin, and half the mint. Season with salt. Stir gently. Set aside.

Prepare the couscous according to the instructions on the package. Stir in the basil, remaining mint, and remaining oil.

Transfer the couscous to a serving dish. Drain the liquid from the zucchini and mix into the couscous. Arrange the zucchini slices over the top. Garnish with the mint and serve.

4 zucchini (courgettes), sliced thinly lengthwise
1/3 cup (90 ml) extra-virgin olive oil
2 tablespoons white wine vinegar
2 shallots, thinly sliced
1 teaspoon cumin seeds
2 sprigs mint, finely chopped
Salt
1½ cups (300 g) precooked couscous
1¼ cups (310 ml) boiling water
3 sprigs basil, torn
Mint leaves, to garnish

Baked Polenta
with ricotta and tomatoes

Bring the water to a boil with the salt. Gradually sprinkle in the polenta while stirring continuously with a large balloon whisk to stop lumps from forming. Cook over a low heat, stirring continuously for about 45 minutes.

Preheat the oven to 350°F (180°C/gas 4). Press the ricotta through a fine mesh strainer.

Heat the oil and butter in a large frying pan over medium heat. Add the onion and sauté until softened, 3–4 minutes. Add the parsley and tomatoes. Mix well. Season with salt and pepper. Simmer over low for 15 minutes.

Turn the polenta out onto a cutting board and let cool. Slice the polenta and arrange a layer in an oiled baking dish. Add half the ricotta and spoon one-third of the sauce over the top. Sprinkle with pecorino. Add another layer of polenta, the remaining ricotta, and half of the remaining sauce. Sprinkle with pecorino and then cover with the remaining polenta. Cover with the remaining sauce and sprinkle with the remaining pecorino.

Bake until the top is golden brown, 20–25 minutes. Let stand for 5–10 minutes before serving.

- 1½ quarts (1.5 liters) cold water
- 1 tablespoon coarse salt
- 2⅓ cups (350 g) polenta (stoneground cornmeal)
- 8 oz (250 g) fresh ricotta cheese, drained
- 3 tablespoons extra-virgin olive oil
- 3 tablespoons butter
- 1 medium onion, finely chopped
- 3 tablespoons finely chopped parsley
- 1 (14-oz/400 g) can tomatoes, with juice
- Freshly ground black pepper
- ½ cup (60 g) freshly grated pecorino or Parmesan cheese

EGGS & CHEESE

Fiery Eggs
with tomatoes

Sauté the onion and garlic in the oil in a large frying pan over medium heat until softened, about 5 minutes.

Stir in the tomatoes and chile pepper. Season with salt and pepper. Simmer for 5 minutes.

Break the eggs into the pan with the tomatoes. Cook until the whites are set but the yolks are still slightly runny, 7–10 minutes.

Serve hot with freshly baked crusty bread.

1 onion, finely chopped
$^1/_4$ cup (60 ml) extra-virgin olive oil
1 clove garlic, finely chopped
2 lb (1 kg) cherry tomatoes, cut in half
1 fresh red chile pepper, seeded and finely chopped
Salt and freshly ground black pepper
6 eggs
Freshly baked crusty bread, to serve

Scrambled Eggs
with zucchini and tomatoes

Sauté the garlic in half the butter and the oil in a large frying pan over medium heat until pale gold, 3–4 minutes. Add the zucchini and sauté over medium heat for 3 minutes. Stir in the tomatoes and simmer for 5 minutes. Discard the garlic. Season with salt and pepper. Set aside.

Beat the eggs in a large bowl. Melt the remaining butter in a large frying pan over medium heat. Add the eggs and stir constantly until set, 3–4 minutes. Season with pepper.

Transfer the eggs to a heated serving dish. Top with the zucchini and tomatoes. Sprinkle with the basil and serve at once.

2 cloves garlic, lightly crushed but whole
⅓ cup (90 g) butter
¼ cup (60 ml) extra-virgin olive oil
4 zucchini (courgettes),cut in small cubes
4 tomatoes, peeled and chopped
Salt and freshly ground black pepper
8 eggs, lightly beaten
2 tablespoons coarsely chopped basil, to garnish

SERVES 2–4

PREPARATION 20 min

COOKING 20–25 min

DIFFICULTY level I

Egg Curry

Sauté the onion in the ghee in a large frying pan over medium heat until golden brown, about 10 minutes.

Add the ginger, garlic, salt, garam masala, coriander seeds, and chile pepper and fry for 2 minutes. Stir in the tomatoes and simmer for 5 minutes. Add the cilantro. Add the eggs and cook over low heat until the sauce thickens, about 5 minutes.

Serve hot with boiled basmati rice.

I onion, finely chopped
I tablespoon ghee (clarified butter)
I tablespoon finely chopped ginger
I clove garlic, finely sliced
I teaspoon salt
I teaspoon garam masala
I teaspoon coriander seeds
$\frac{1}{2}$ teaspoon chile powder
I (14-oz/400-g) can tomatoes, with juice
I small bunch fresh cilantro (coriander), finely chopped
4 hard-boiled eggs, peeled but whole
Freshly cooked basmati rice, to serve

SERVES 4–6

PREPARATION 45 min

COOKING 25–30 min

DIFFICULTY level I

Cheese Crêpes
with vegetables

Prepare the crêpes. Preheat the oven to 400°F (200°C/gas 6.)

Sauté the carrot, zucchini, and leek in 2 tablespoons of oil in a frying pan until golden, about 5 minutes. Transfer to a baking dish.

Beat the ricotta, egg, pecorino, and ½ cup (60 g) of Parmesan in a large bowl. Spread the mixture over the crêpes and roll up loosely. Place half the crêpes on top of the vegetables in the baking dish.

Sauté the garlic in the remaining oil in a large frying pan until pale gold. Add the spinach and sauté for 7 minutes.

Transfer to the baking dish and arrange the remaining crêpes on top. Drizzle with the cream, season with pepper, and sprinkle with the remaining Parmesan.

Bake until golden, 8–10 minutes. Serve hot.

I quantity crêpes (see page 302),
 made without the fresh herbs

Filling
I carrot, cut into matchsticks
2 zucchini (courgettes,) cut into matchsticks
White of I leek, very finely sliced
¼ cup (60 ml) extra-virgin olive oil
1⅔ cups (400 g) ricotta cheese, drained
I egg
1¾ cups (200) g freshly grated pecorino
 cheese
¾ cup (90 g) freshly grated Parmesan
 cheese
I clove garlic, finely chopped
14 oz (400 g) spinach leaves, blanched
3 tablespoons heavy (double) cream
Freshly ground black pepper

SERVES 4

PREPARATION 45 min

COOKING 1 h

DIFFICULTY level 3

Asparagus Spirals
with cheese

Prepare the crêpes.

Filling: Cook the spinach and asparagus in salted boiling water until tender. Drain and chop finely. Mix the spinach, asparagus, goat cheese, and ricotta in a large bowl. Season with salt and nutmeg.

Spread the filling over the crêpes and carefully roll up. Cut each crêpe into 1 inch (2.5 cm) slices.

Preheat the oven to 400°F (200°C/gas 6). Butter a baking dish.

Place the slices of crêpe in the baking dish. Drizzle with the cream, dot with the butter, and sprinkle with the Parmesan. Bake until browned, about 15 minutes. Serve hot.

1 quantity crêpes (see page 302) made without the fresh herbs

Filling
14 oz (400 g) fresh spinach leaves, stalks removed
1 lb (500 g) tender asparagus spears
$3/4$ cup (180 g) creamy goat cheese
1 cup (250 g) ricotta cheese, drained
Salt
$1/8$ teaspoon freshly grated nutmeg
$2/3$ cup (150 ml) light (single) cream
1 tablespoon butter, cut up
$3/4$ cup (90 g) freshly grated Parmesan cheese

Cheese Crêpes
with zucchini

Crêpes: Mix the flour and milk in a large bowl. Add the eggs and beat until well blended. Beat in the thyme, marjoram, and parsley. Season with salt.

Melt the butter in a small frying pan over medium heat. Pour in just enough batter to cover the bottom of the pan, tilting it so that it thinly covers the surface. Cook until the crêpe is lightly gold on the underside. Use a large spatula to flip and cook the other side. Repeat until all the batter has been used. Stack the cooked crêpes one on top of another in a warm oven.

Preheat the oven to 400°F (200°C/gas 6). Butter a large baking dish.

Ricotta Filling: Sauté the zucchini in the butter in a large frying pan over medium heat until softened, 5–10 minutes.

Add the zucchini flowers, ricotta, pine nuts, nutmeg, salt, and pepper. Simmer for 3 minutes.

Place 2–3 tablespoons of filling in the center of each crêpe. Fold the crêpes in half and then in half again to form triangles.

Arrange the filled crêpes in the prepared baking dish. Pour the cream over the top and sprinkle with the Parmesan.

Cover with aluminum foil and bake for 10 minutes. Remove the foil and bake until the crêpes are crisp and the cheese is golden brown, 8–10 minutes more. Serve hot.

Crêpes
1²⁄₃ cups (250 g) all-purpose (plain) flour
2 cups (500 ml) milk
4 eggs
1 tablespoon finely chopped thyme
1 tablespoon finely chopped marjoram
1 tablespoon finely chopped parsley
¹⁄₄ teaspoon salt
1 tablespoon butter

Ricotta Filling
12 oz (350 g) zucchini (courgettes), cut into rounds
2 tablespoons butter
24 zucchini flowers, carefully washed
1²⁄₃ cups (400 g) ricotta cheese, drained
¹⁄₂ cup (60 g) pine nuts, toasted
¹⁄₄ teaspoon freshly ground nutmeg
Salt and freshly ground black pepper
1¹⁄₄ cups (310 ml) single (light) cream
1 tablespoon freshly grated Parmesan cheese

Savory Cheesecake

SERVES 8

PREPARATION 40 min + 3 h to chill

COOKING 30-35 min

DIFFICULTY level 2

Preheat the oven to 350°F (180°C/gas 4).

Place the toast in a plastic bag and use a bottle to crush it into fine bread crumbs.

Set aside 1 tablespoon of butter and melt the rest in a small frying pan over low heat. Add the bread crumbs and cook until the butter has been absorbed. Add the water.

Butter the base and sides of an 11-inch (28-cm) springform pan. Line the base with waxed paper.

Firmly press the bread crumb mixture into the base and sides of the pan.

Beat the ricotta, soft cheese, Parmesan, eggs, and salt and pepper in a large bowl until creamy. Spoon the cream over the crumb base, smoothing the surface. Knock the pan on a work surface two or three times to remove air bubbles.

Cut the tomatoes in half and arrange on the top of the cheesecake, pressing them in slightly.

Bake until browned on top, 25–30 minutes. Let cool completely. Refrigerate for 3 hours before serving.

8 oz (250 g) whole-wheat (wholemeal) toast
1/2 cup (125 g) butter, cut up
1/4 cup (60 ml) cold water
1 2/3 cups (400 g) ricotta cheese, drained
1 cup (250 g) soft fresh cheese
1/2 cup (60 g) freshly grated Parmesan cheese
3 eggs
Salt and freshly ground black pepper
5 oz (150 g) cherry tomatoes

SERVES 6

PREPARATION 40 min

COOKING 20 min

DIFFICULTY level 2

Pancakes
with two cheeses

Pancakes: Mix the water and garbanzo bean flour in a small bowl until well blended.

Beat the eggs and milk in a large bowl until frothy. Mix in the flour, butter, and garbanzo flour mixture until smooth. Season with salt.

Grease a small frying pan with oil. Pour 2 tablespoons of the batter into the pan, tilting it so that the batter covers the surface. Cook until the pancake is light golden on the underside. Use a large spatula to flip the pancake and cook until golden on the other side. Repeat until all the batter has been used.

Preheat the oven to 400°F (200°C/gas 60). Butter a large baking dish.

Cheese Filling: Mix the ricotta, goat cheese, ½ cup (60 g) of Parmesan, marjoram, parsley, and garlic in a large bowl. Season with salt and pepper.

Spread the pancakes with the filling and roll them up tightly. Place the pancakes seamside down in the baking dish. Sprinkle with the remaining Parmesan and dot with the butter.

Bake until browned, 8–10 minutes. Serve warm on a bed of arugula.

Pancakes
⅔ cup (150 ml) water
⅔ cup (100 g) garbanzo bean (chickpea) flour
2 eggs
⅓ cup (90 ml) milk
⅓ cup (50 g) all-purpose (plain) flour
1 tablespoon butter, melted
Salt

Cheese Filling
1 cup (250 g) ricotta cheese
⅔ cup (150 g) creamy goat cheese
¾ cup (90 g) freshly grated Parmesan cheese
1 tablespoon finely chopped marjoram
1 tablespoon finely chopped parsley
1 clove garlic, finely chopped
Salt and freshly ground black pepper
1 tablespoon butter
1 bunch arugula (rocket), to serve

Broccoli Omelet

Clean the broccoli. Dice the stalk into bite-sized pieces and break the head into small florets. Cook in salted, boiling water until tender but still crunchy, about 5–7 minutes. Drain well and set aside.

Combine the eggs, soy sauce, chilies, peanuts, and parsley in a bowl with the broccoli.

Heat the oil in a large frying pan and sauté the garlic and spring onions until softened, 3–4 minutes. Pour in the egg mixture and stir well. Cover and cook over medium-low heat until the bottom of the omelet is lightly browned.

Brown the top of the omelet under the broiler (grill) and serve hot or at room temperature.

12 oz (300 g) broccoli
5 eggs
3 teaspoons light soy sauce
2 medium red chilies, finely chopped
2 oz (60 g) finely chopped roasted peanuts
4 tablespoons finely chopped parsley
2 tablespoons extra-virgin olive oil
2 cloves garlic, finely chopped
6 spring onions, finely chopped

Scrambled Eggs
mexican style

Heat the oil in a large frying pan.

Beat the eggs until frothy, then add the chilies, onion, cilantro, and salt.

Pour the mixture into the hot oil and cook until the eggs are softly scrambled, stirring them with a fork so that they cook evenly.

To serve, spoon the beans onto a deep platter and top with the scrambled eggs.

$\frac{1}{2}$ cup (125 ml) extra-virgin olive oil

16 eggs

2 green chilies, finely chopped

1 white onion, finely chopped

6 tablespoons finely chopped cilantro (coriander)

Salt

3 cups (600 g) cooked black beans

Cheese Soufflé

Preheat the oven to 350°F (180°C/gas 4).

Lightly beat the egg yolks in a large bowl. Add the milk, butter, and mustard to the eggs and mix well. Stir in the bread crumbs and cheese and season with the salt and pepper.

Beat the egg whites until stiff with a dash of salt and fold them into the mixture.

Pour into a buttered soufflé dish and bake until well risen, brown on top, and set in the middle, 30–40 minutes. Serve at once.

4 eggs, separated

1¼ cups (300 ml) milk, warmed

1 tablespoon butter, melted

1 teaspoon mustard

3 oz (90 g) fresh bread crumbs

4 oz (125 g) freshly grated Cheddar or Emmental cheese

Salt and freshly ground black pepper

Zucchini Frittata

Sauté the garlic in the oil in a large frying pan over medium heat until pale gold. Add the zucchini and sauté for 5–7 minutes, or until tender. Season with salt and pepper.

Beat the eggs and cheese in a medium bowl. Pour the egg mixture into the pan and cook for 2–3 minutes, or until the egg has almost cooked.

Slide the frittata onto a plate, turn onto another plate, then slide it back into the pan to cook the other side. Cook until golden brown and the egg is cooked through, 2–3 minutes.

Transfer the frittata to a serving dish and serve hot.

- 1 clove garlic, finely chopped
- 3 tablespoons extra-virgin olive oil
- 2 lb (1 kg) zucchini (courgettes), cut into short, thin lengths
- Salt and freshly ground black pepper
- 6 large eggs
- 1/2 cup (60 g) freshly grated pecorino or Parmesan cheese

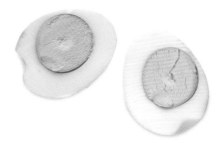

Curried Eggs
with apple

Melt the butter in a medium-sized heavy-bottomed saucepan over medium heat. Add the onion and sauté until softened, 3–4 minutes.

Add the apple and sauté for 3–4 minutes more. Sprinkle with the flour, curry powder, and cumin and stir for 2–3 minutes.

Slowly add the stock, stirring continuously to ensure a smooth texture. Simmer for a few minutes and then add the quartered eggs.

Sprinkle with the parsley and serve hot.

¹⁄₄ cup (60 g) butter
1 large onion, finely chopped
1 cooking apple, peeled and diced
1 oz (30 g) all-purpose (plain) flour
1–2 tablespoons curry powder
1 teaspoon ground cumin
2¹⁄₂ cups (625 ml) boiling vegetable stock
6 hard-boiled eggs, shelled and cut in half
1 tablespoon finely chopped parsley

SERVES 8–10

PREPARATION 20 min

COOKING 10 min

DIFFICULTY level 1

Cheese Savories

Preheat the oven to 400°F (200°C/gas 6). Oil two baking sheets

Place the flour and baking powder in a medium bowl. Rub the butter into the flour, then add the cheese. Season with salt and pepper and stir in enough of the milk to make a stiff dough.

Roll out on a lightly floured work surface into a very thin sheet. Use a cookie cutter or small glass to cut into rounds and a sharp knife to cut into straws.

Place the savories on the prepared baking sheets and bake until golden brown, about 10 minutes.

Serve hot or at room temperature.

²/₃ cup (100 g) all-purpose flour
1 teaspoon baking powder
¹/₄ cup (60 g) butter
3 oz (90 g) freshly grated Cheddar
    or Emmental cheese
Salt and and freshly ground black pepper
¹/₂ cup (125 ml) milk

Index